THE ART LAW PRIMER

THE
ART LAW
PRIMER

A Manual for Visual Artists

LINDA F. PINKERTON
JOHN T. GUARDALABENE

NICK LYONS BOOKS
Nick Lyons • Peter Burford
Publishers

Printed in the United States of America

10 9 8 7 6 5 5 4 3 2 1

Library of Congress Cataloging-in-Publication Data

Pinkerton, Linda F.
    The art law primer.

    Includes index.
        1. Artists—Legal status, laws, etc.—United States.
    2. Artists' contracts—United States.   3. Copyright—
    Art—United States.   I. Guardalabene, John T.   II. Title.
    KF390.A7P56   1988   346.7304′82   88–23047
    ISBN 1–55821–002–4   347.306482

To Toni, Michael, Skeezix and Guido

CONTENTS

INTRODUCTION

More and more laws affecting artists are being written every year. Some clarify artists' existing rights; others create new ones. Many of these laws also impose certain obligations on artists. Today, more than ever, an ounce of prevention is worth a pound of legal cure. Every artist can and should know the legal rights available to protect him and his work, as well as the rights of the other parties in his relationships. Understanding legal concepts will enable a professional artist to negotiate favorable agreements, protect his reputation and generally be regarded as a professional by others in the marketplace.

This book sets out the basics of the areas of law affecting most visual artists in the United States. The law changes rapidly and varies from state to state, but emerging trends and established principles governing the subjects covered can be mastered easily and used for consultation with an attorney. We have endeavored to encourage preventive action rather than emphasize remedies. Above all, we have limited the text to the readable basics in order not to confuse the reader with legal details and intricacies which may not apply to his particular situation. For this reason, an expert should be consulted when a complex legal problem does arise.

Chapter 1 deals with federal copyright law, which protects original works of art. The second chapter addresses contract law and some typical contractual relationships most visual artists face. The law governing relationships with art dealers and publishers is covered in Chapter 3.

Reproductions and publications are covered in Chapter 4. Business necessities such as leases and taxes are discussed in Chapters 5 and 6. Chapter 7 considers moral right. For artists and/or works entering the United States from other countries, Chapter 8 examines the United States' immigration and customs laws. Chapter 9 provides some guidelines for getting legal help. The last chapter includes miscellaneous practical considerations.

Our goal has been to produce a practical guide for visual artists who do not wish to master the law but simply want to understand their fundamental rights and obligations. This book is not a substitute for the legal advice an attorney can provide on specific legal problems. If you think you see a legal problem emerging, we recommend you consult an atttorney sooner rather than later.

Even as we are preparing the final manuscript, Congress and various state legislatures are making major changes in the laws covered in the text. Although we describe the direction in which the law appears to be heading, we urge the reader to contact his local or state arts organization about new laws affecting specific transactions. As a final note, our references to members of one sex are intended to serve as a reference to either. We use "he" and "him" only as shorthand.

Linda F. Pinkerton
John T. Guardalabene
August, 1988

THE ART LAW PRIMER

1

COPYRIGHT

Consider the following facts: You are an experienced architect who has recently taken up painting. You are quite pleased with the results of your first efforts, and invite a few friends over to your studio to show them your work. One friend admires a particular canvas and asks if he can photograph the work and use the print for his personal Christmas card. You have no objection. This is a good friend and you know he would not commercially exploit the painting. Several months later you receive one of your friend's cards. About a hundred other people also receive the card.

The following year you see on the cover of a magazine a painting that looks suspiciously similar to the painting you permitted your friend to use on his Christmas card. When you look inside you find that the cover painting is credited to someone you never heard of and, in addition, the illustration of the cover bears a copyright notice. You call your friend and ask if he knows the person credited with your painting. Your friend admits that he sent that person a Christmas card but says he knows nothing about the magazine cover.

You then telephone the person claiming credit for your painting. He tells you that he did not use your painting but did make his own copy, with some changes, for the magazine. When you complain about the use of your work in this manner, the other person says there was no copyright notice on the card and that as far as he is concerned the

1

painting is in the public domain. So, he concludes, it is your problem, not his. According to him, you should have required your friend to put a copyright notice on the Christmas card. Your response is that he has broken the law and that you want compensation for the use of your painting. The other person laughs and hangs up.

What are your rights? Is there anything you can do about the unauthorized copying and use of your painting? What if your painting was copyrighted but your friend's card did not bear a copyright notice?

The possible twists and turns in the copyright world seem endless. Yet, with a minimum amount of effort beyond meticulous consistency, you can avoid most copyright problems. The major exception is the pirate, a person who intentionally undertakes to infringe your copyright despite the fact that you have fully complied with the law. Even there we have some potentially powerful legal tools. So please read on. We think you will be able to answer the questions we posed above, and many others, for yourself after reading this chapter.

THE COPYRIGHT CONCEPT

Copyright is a system of personal property rights under United States federal law which protects copyright owners from the unauthorized reproduction of the work to which the copyright is attached. Copyright applies to original works of authorship including, in addition to works of visual arts, literature, drama, music, choreography and pantomime. Although our primary concern in this book is with the visual arts, many artists' works consist of a combination of media. Some artists are also authors who might illustrate their own texts, or add text to accompany their visual works. Other artists might create mixed visual and musical works. The more complex the mixture of media, the more complicated the copyright issues are likely to be. While we cannot address all the copyright implications of mixed-media works of art, we at least hope to alert you to the potential problems. These include your own possible violation of other artists' copyrights, as well as protecting your own copyrighted works from the unauthorized use by others.

Copyrights are often confused with trademarks, but they are very different legal concepts. When you produce a painting, the copyright law protects your creative effort at the time the painting comes into being. You need do nothing further with the painting in order to retain the protection of your copyright. A trademark, however, is a device for identifying goods or services. It has no meaning apart from the goods or services associated with it; and a trademark cannot be registered or retained if it is not used. A trademark is not automatic as is copyright.

Some items are eligible for both copyright and trademark protection. Yet, some design elements or trademarks may be too basic to satisfy the minimal originality requirements of the copyright law. Moreover, the trademark laws usually are far more important to a trademark owner than any copyright that he might own in the trademark design. Nevertheless, while names or titles ordinarily are not entitled to copyright protection, the graphic portions of trademarks may be copyrighted. If you are intending to use your own copyrighted artwork as part of a trademark for goods you are producing or services you will provide, we encourage you to consult a lawyer who is experienced in trademark issues.

A copyright is not something that you, the artist, must apply for. Copyright exists in the work of art and is a direct result of the creative act. Except for special situations involving "works made for hire" (which we will talk about later), the copyright comes into being and belongs to the artist (or more than one artist if the work is a collaboration) when the work of art comes into being. But the copyright is not the same thing as the physical object to which it is attached. As we shall see, you do not necessarily transfer your copyright along with the physical work of art at the time of sale, lease, loan, gift or other conveyance. Unless you expressly agree in writing that you are transferring your copyright, you, as creator of the work or art, retain ownership of the copyright and all related legal rights.

The copyright is inherent in the physical expression of the work of art, as long as the work has a reasonable degree of permanence and form. This is true even if the artwork is an evolving one. At any stage along the way (regardless of your medium) copyright will exist for the work. In fact, a work-in-progress could give rise to numerous copyrights. For example, photographs or casts of a sculpture at various stages of development could be individually copyrighted. However, some works of art are not eligible for copyright because, in the language of the copyright law, they are not "fixed in a tangible medium of expression." For example, ice sculptures or sand sculptures ordinarily cannot be copyrighted because their forms are only temporary.

For most visual artists, however, deciding whether or not a work of art can be copyrighted is not a problem. Nevertheless, if you are in doubt about whether a specific work of art can be copyrighted, you should seek the advice of a copyright specialist. A number of states (including California) provide copyright protection for works that are not eligible for federal copyright. While the extent of protection is substantially less than that provided by federal statute, state law might still offer sufficient leverage to stop someone from copying or reproducing your work.

You do not have to do anything to obtain a copyright in your own work of art. Neither putting the little "c" in the circle nor registering your work of art creates the copyright. You, the artist, own the copyright simply because you created the work of art. The copyright is your property until you decide to part with it, unless you inadvertently cast your work into the public domain. Nevertheless, the little "c" in the circle and copyright registration are important. Both are relatively simple procedures which we will describe in some detail later in the chapter.

The main sources of copyright law are federal statutes. The current national law is the Copyright Act of 1976. There were many important changes in copyright as a result of this law; nevertheless, the old Copyright Act of 1909 still applies to works of art produced prior to 1978. For artists who have been active before 1978 and beyond, the old and the new copyright laws are relevant. In our discussion of copyright we will describe the differences between the two acts so you will be able to understand the distinctions between your rights (and how you can lose them) under both laws.

THE EXCLUSIVE RIGHTS

The property rights of a copyright owner under the United States copyright law actually consist of a group of five separate rights known as the "exclusive rights." They are: 1) the right to reproduce copyrighted work; 2) the right to create derivative works based on the copyrighted work; 3) the right to distribute copies of the copyrighted work; 4) the right to perform the work; and 5) the right to display the work. Clearly, the value of these individual exclusive rights will vary greatly from one artist to another. For example, the right to perform one's work may have limited value for a graphic artist, since the only works of the visual arts this right applies to are motion pictures and other audiovisual works. Nevertheless, an artist as copyright owner controls these exclusive rights and may deal with each independently.

Let's look at the exclusive rights individually. For an artist the reproduction right is often the most economically valuable of the exclusive rights. Without the copyright owner's permission, no one may duplicate a copyrighted work in any manner. (There is one exception to this rule, known as "fair use," which we will talk about later in the chapter.) This includes reproducing the work in another medium. For example, an unauthorized pencil drawing of a photograph would constitute an infringement of the reproduction right. So, too, would the unauthorized production of a toy based upon a cartoon character.

Photographic reproduction of works of art is a frequent source of infringement. The copyright owner's permission must be obtained before an artwork may be reproduced in a photograph. To include a photograph of a sculpture in a book which purports to be a survey of contemporary sculpture would constitute infringement unless permission to reproduce the work has been given by the copyright owner.

The right to make derivative works, also known as the adaptation right, generally overlaps with the reproduction right. The copyright law defines a derivative work as one "based upon one or more pre-existing works, such as translation, musical arrangement, dramatization, fictionalization, motion picture version, sound recording, art reproduction, abridgement, condensation, or any other form in which a work may be recast, transformed or adapted.'' The possible forms which adaptations of an artist's work may take are limited only by the imagination. Returning to the contemporary sculpture mentioned above, a second sculptor who attempts to produce his own original copy of the first sculptor's work infringes both the reproduction and the adaptation rights. The reproduction right is infringed because the copyright owner (the artist) did not give his permission for the work to be copied in any manner. The adaptation right is infringed because the copy is not an exact duplicate.

Infringements of the adaptation right might also occur when a work of art, or a portion of that work, is incorporated in any form into another work. For example, a collage which incorporates original painting by an artist along with a copyrighted photograph by another artist very well may constitute an infringement of copyright where permission to utilize the photograph has not been obtained. Even the incorporation of a well-known detail from one work of art into a second work of art without permission may constitute an infringement.

The performance right does not apply to the traditional visual arts. The 1976 Copyright law limits this right to literary, musical, dramatic, and choreographic works, pantomimes, and motion pictures and other audiovisual works. In the event it were possible to ''perform'' a painting, no infringement would occur because the copyright owner of the painting would not have an exclusive performance right. For example, it may be possible to create a human tableau or a three-dimensional setting of certain paintings or sculptures. While the ''performance'' of the visual work of art would not constitute an infringement, there may be an infringement of the adaptation right. If the performance were substantially similar to the original work of art, it is arguable that the performance is a derivative work and thus an infringement of that right.

The final exclusive right, the right to display, is of obvious importance to all visual artists. To display a copyrighted work means to show the original of that work or any reproduction or copy in public, either directly or by means of a device such as film, slides or television images.

The exclusive rights provided under copyright law, however, are not absolute. There are limitations, three of which are particularly important to visual artists:

1) The owner of a lawful copy of a work (including the original) has the right to sell or otherwise transfer ownership of the work he owns, even though that person does not own the copyright to the work. This may sound like common sense, but without this provision in the law many collectors of modern art could be subject to legal action for infringement of the copyright owner's distribution right.

2) The owner of a lawful copy of a work (including the original) is also entitled to display this work publicly, either directly or by some device, as long as the display occurs in the same location as the work itself. For example, a gallery exhibiting the work of the prominent nihil-modernist painter, Nosevll Tai, may also present a slide show of Tar'o paintings on the gallery premises. Similarly, a museum which does not own the copyright to a painting in its collection may televise a lecture about the artist, including the image of the painting, as long as the transmission occurs only in the museum building.

3) Fair use: Under the current copyright law, unauthorized reproduction of copyrighted works under certain circumstances does not constitute infringement of copyright. Among the purposes which might qualify as "fair use" are "criticism, comment, news reporting, teaching (including multiple copies for classroom use), scholarship or research."

Whether a particular use will be considered "fair" ultimately depends upon the facts of the situation. But the Copyright Act does provide some guidelines. The following factors are not conclusive, but they still are useful for both users and copyright owners in considering whether an infringement might or might not occur: (1) the purpose and character of the use, including whether such use is of a commercial nature or is for nonprofit educational purposes; (2) the nature of the copyrighted work; (3) the amount and substantiality of the portion used in relation to the copyrighted work as a whole; and (4) the effect of the use upon the potential market for or value of the copyrighted work.

Although there are no stated limitations on the methods of reproduction or the kinds of works which may be reproduced under the "fair use" concept, the most common form of reproduction contemplated is photocopying for classroom use. While this situation more frequently concerns works in print, visual artists can also be affected.

PUBLICATION

Although it is true that a copyright comes into being with the fixing of the creative act in a tangible form, there are circumstances when the artist must take action to protect his copyright. The most important situation of this kind is when the work of art is "published." The current copyright law requires notice of copyright to be placed upon all "published" copies of the work. While the same is true of the 1909 Act, the consequences of failing to affix a copyright notice to the work at the time of "publication" are drastically different between the old and the new law. Under the old law, a work of art would permanently fall into the public domain if, at the time of "publication," a proper copyright notice was not affixed. Under the current law, it is much more difficult to inject a work of art into the public domain, although it can be done. You can avoid this problem altogether by complying with the requirement of the 1976 Act that a work subject to copyright display the copyright notice at the time of publication.

The term "publication" in the copyright context is a technical one and does not necessarily imply the existence of a reproduction of the work of art. The copyright law defines publication as: "the distribution of copies . . . of a work to the public by sale or other transfer of ownership or rental, lease or lending . . ." or "the offering to distribute [such copies] for purposes of further distribution, public performance or public display."

You undoubtedly noticed the use of the word "copies" in the definition of "publication." "Copy" is also a technical copyright term which differs from the everyday meaning of the word. As strange as it may seem, the term "copy" in the copyright context includes the original as well as reproductions.

Generally speaking, publication occurs when you sell, lease, loan or give away your work to the general public. But for many artists this definition does not address the normal manner in which they sell or otherwise transfer possession of their art. For the artist who sells single original works of art from his own studio or through a gallery or similar type of commercial environment, the determination of whether the work has been "published" for copyright purposes may depend on whether the work was created before or after January 1, 1978.

Under the 1909 Copyright Act (which applies to works created prior to 1978), publication for copyright purposes probably occurred whenever a work of art was publicly sold or otherwise made available to the public through a gallery or auction house. Even where the work was not offered for sale, but merely exhibited to the public, there is a good possibility that "publication" occurred.

Under the 1976 Act the offer to sell or otherwise transfer ownership or an interest in a work of art to the public may also constitute "publication." However, under the current law it is clear that exhibition of a work of art does not in and of itself constitute "publication" unless there is a corresponding offer to the public to transfer an interest in the work. So, if you have a previously "unpublished" work exhibited in a museum or other noncommercial exhibition, "publication" will not occur simply because your work is exhibited. Under both the old and the new law, private sales out of an artist's studio would not result in "publication."

But what if someone photographs or otherwise copies your "unpublished" work while it is exhibited in a noncommercial setting but without a copyright notice affixed to it? Since your work is protected by copyright from the moment of creation, and because you have no legal obligation to affix a copyright notice prior to "publication," anyone who copies your work under those circumstances is infringing your copyright. That is a violation of the copyright law.

COPYRIGHT NOTICE

When a copyright notice is affixed to a work of art (or any other work that can be copyrighted) the form of the notice must comply with the law. The elements of a proper copyright notice are: first, the c-in-the-circle [©] or the word "copyright" or the abbreviation "copr."; second, the year of first publication; and third, the name of the copyright owner, or an abbreviation by which the name can be recognized, or a generally known alternative designation of the owner. So, there are six acceptable ways for the artist Art Liveson, better known as Gaucho, to show a correct copyright notice for one of his works first published in 1989:

1) © 1989 Art Liveson   4) © 1989 Gaucho
2) Copyright 1989 Art Liveson   5) Copyright 1989 Gaucho
3) Copr. 1989 Art Liveson   6) Copr. 1989 Gaucho

Some artists, such as fine art jewelers, have a symbol or a mark by which they are known. If Art Liveson had such a symbol, he could have substituted the symbol as an alternative designation to "Art Liveson" or "Gaucho." In addition, the copyright law would permit Mr. Liveson to omit the year from the copyright notice if he were reproducing one of his copyrighted paintings on any utilitarian item such as a toy or a greeting card. The publishing trade often uses "Copyright © 1989 by Art Liveson Press" for notice purposes. Although this form of notice is redundant and unnecessary, it is probably used to insure maximum protection under the Universal Copyright Convention (see page 20).

What if you decide to affix your copyright notice at a time prior to first publication? Don't worry. In fact, this is a very good safeguard in the event there is ever any ambiguity about what event constitutes "publication" of your work. Use the current year for notice purposes. The only real danger in using the wrong date is where the date on the notice is a year or more later than the actual year of first publication.

The copyright law also requires that notice be placed in such a way as to give reasonable notice of the copyright claim. Does that mean an artist, in effect, must deface the work of art in order to comply with the law? No. Notice may be placed on the back or front of a two-dimensional art object or on any other material to which the artwork is permanently housed. For a painting, copyright notice is valid if the notice is securely affixed to the back of the painting, either directly (with paint, ink, engraving or whatever) or by means of a firmly attached label. Putting the notice on the frame is not satisfactory. A three-dimensional work must display its notice somewhere on a visible portion of the work. The notice would be invalid if it were placed on the bottom or inside of a sculpture.

As we mentioned earlier, for works created prior to 1978, failure to affix the copyright notice at the time of "publication" resulted in the work being forever thrown into the public domain. When a work enters the public domain, it may be copied by anybody, and the artist receives no royalties or other form of financial remuneration. The result can mean the loss of a great deal of money to an artist. The best known example of a popular work of art which fell into the public domain at the time of publication is Robert Indiana's LOVE design. This graphic design has been reproduced in seemingly endless numbers of copies. But Mr. Indiana has no control over who reproduces the work and he receives no license fees or royalties from these reproductions. The work was published without a copyright notice.

The problem of forfeiting copyright may at first appear important only to artists who produce multiples. But many artists, particularly after achieving a measure of commercial success, produce works that are reproduced in books, brochures, postcards, exhibition catalogues and posters. Reproduction of a work in any of these, or similar, formats constitutes a copy of the work for copyright purposes. If "publication" of a reproduction of a work occurred prior to 1978 and neither the underlying artwork nor the reproduction had a legally correct copyright notice at the time of "publication," the artwork itself as well as the reproduction would have been permanently thrown into the public domain.

The current copyright law is more lenient. If Mr. Indiana had produced his design in the 1980s instead of the 1960s, the lack of copyright notice could have been corrected. Under the current law, if you publicly distribute only a small number of copies without the copyright notice, you are in no danger of losing your copyright. In fact, under those circumstances you don't have to do anything at all to protect your copyright. But if you have distributed a large number of copies (the government does not specify how many that is) without the notice, you must register your copyright with the Copyright Office within five years and make a reasonable effort to affix a notice to all copies yet to be distributed. Failure to do this will cause your work to fall into the public domain.

REGISTRATION

Copyright registration is not a pre-requisite for obtaining or maintaining a valid copyright. Nevertheless, it does confer some valuable benefits. For example, you will not be able to bring a lawsuit for infringement unless you have first registered your work. If you register within three months of publication of the work, you are eligible to recover attorneys' fees and statutory damages if you bring a lawsuit for copyright infringement. Perhaps most important, as we stated above, registration within five years is the only way to prevent forfeiture of copyright if you or someone acting with your authorization publish more than a small number of copies without the copyright notice.

Copyright registration is a very simple procedure which you can do yourself. The Copyright Office of the United States government produces several different forms corresponding to the type of material being registered. Form VA (which we have attached in the Appendix) is used for works of visual arts, Form TX is used for non-dramatic literary works (for example, books and exhibition catalogues), Form PA is used for performing arts works and Form SR is used for sound recordings.

To obtain forms, write to the Publications Section, LM-455, Copyright Office, Library of Congress, Washington D.C. 20559. The forms are self-explanatory. To register: 1) mail the completed form appropriate to the medium of your artwork accompanied by the ten-dollar registration fee and, usually, two copies of the copyrighted work. You are not required to create duplicates of a one-of-a-kind work of art. Transparencies are generally adequate. For printed materials, except for some limited editions, copies of the actual work are required. Specific information on registration requirements for your medium of art is available from the Copyright Office. That government agency has prepared two publications for owners of copyrights for works of the visual arts: Copyright Office Circular 40, "Copyright Registration for Works of the Visual Arts" and Circular 40a, "Deposit Requirements for Registration Claims to Copyright in Visual Arts Material." These can be obtained by writing to the address listed above for registration forms or calling the twenty-four hour Forms and Publications Hotline at 202-287-9100.

DURATION

Copyrights do not last forever. The duration of a copyright depends upon whether the work was created prior to January 1, 1978. For works of art produced on or after January 1, 1978, copyright duration is determined by the 1976 Copyright Act. The copyright of such works begins at the time the work is created and lasts for the lifetime of the maker of the work plus an additional fifty years. So, for example, if Art Liveson produces a painting in 1980 and dies in 1999, the copyright of the painting will last until 2049. In the case of a joint work of art, the copyright expires fifty years after the death of the last surviving joint author of the work.

The Copyright Act of 1909 governs the duration of copyrights for works created prior to January 1, 1978. Under the old Act, in contrast with the present law, federal copyright protection did not attach to a copyrightable work until the work was "published." When that event occurred, assuming proper notice was affixed, federal copyright protection began and lasted for a term of twenty-eight years. The copyright could then be renewed for another twenty-eight year term if a renewal application was properly made and registered with the Copyright Office. Unless specifically provided otherwise by contract, the renewal term, i.e., the second term of the copyright, reverted to the author of the work. Thus, an artist who sold a copyrighted painting along with the copyright, would have a second chance to benefit from the copyright after the first term of copyright expired. However, failure to file the renewal in a timely manner would cause the work to enter the public domain. The timely renewal requirement still applies to hundreds of thousands of works that were created prior to 1978 and which are still in the first term of copyright.

To make a timely renewal of a copyright for a work whose first term ends after January 1, 1978, the application must be made to the Copyright Office and registered within a one-year period preceding the end of the twenty-eighth calendar year after the year in which the copyrighted work was first published. So, a copyrighted work that was first published in 1961 has a first term that will expire on December 31, 1989. The application for renewal must be made sometime between January 1 and December 31, 1989. The renewal deadline was different under the old law. For a work whose first term expired prior to January 1, 1978, the renewal must have been made within the twelve months preceding the twenty-eighth anniversary of the exact date of first publication.

Where a copyright is jointly owned, valid renewal for all co-owners is accomplished where even one co-owner renews in his own name. If an artist dies before applying for a renewal term of copyright, the right to renew passes to a surviving spouse and children. Remember that renewal applies only to works that are governed by the old law. Renewal forms are available from the Copyright Office. Renewal for a second term will now provide an additional forty-seven years of copyright protection.

Here are some illustrations of how to determine whether a valid copyright exists for works produced before 1978. In 1945, Paul Sopasic produced a clay model for an intended bronze casting. Brochures which included a photo of the clay model were widely distributed. Neither the brochure nor the photo bore a copyright notice. Did a copyright attach to Mr. Sopasic's work, and, if so, when did it expire? The distribution of the photo of the clay model probably constituted "publication" of the artwork. Since there was no notice attached to the brochure, the photo or the clay model at the time of publication, all three items entered the public domain. Worse yet, the bronze based on the clay model also probably entered the public domain. This illustration is derived from the true case of the monumental Chicago Picasso, "Untitled, 1967," which a federal court determined to be in the public domain.

Now we'll change the facts slightly. In 1945 Paul Sopasic produced the clay model we described earlier. This time the model bore a proper copyright notice. In 1974 Mr. Sopasic filed for a renewal of his copyright. What is the result? The clay model falls into the public domain. Mr. Sopasic filed for renewal in the twenty-ninth year. He had to file within the twelve months prior to the twenty-eighth anniversary of first publication, to avoid forfeiting copyright. Had the renewal been filed by the anniversary date of first publication in 1973, he would have been entitled to a second copyright term of twenty-eight years. The copyright then would have lasted until 2001. (As of January 1, 1978, the renewal period would have been automatically extended to 2018.)

Now assume Guido Carpaccio produced a painting in 1975 and that he affixed proper copyright notice at the time of "publication." How long will his copyright last? The first term of his copyright ends in 2003 (that is, after twenty-eight years). If Guido files for renewal between January 1 and December 31, 2003, he will obtain a second term for the copyright lasting until 2050. The reason is that the new Copyright Act adds nineteen years to the length of copyright for works created prior to 1978. This is how you compute it: if you have a copyright in its first term as of January 1, 1978, and you make a timely renewal, your second term will last forty-seven years instead of twenty-eight years. If your copyright is already in its second term as of January 1, 1978, you automatically receive an extra nineteen years on the duration of your copyright.

What happens to a work of art that was created prior to 1978 but not published until 1978 or later? Generally, such a work will receive the same copyright duration as works created after January 1, 1978, *i.e.* life of the artist plus fifty years. But what if the artist died fifty or more years prior to 1978? Then the artwork will have copyright protection until 2002 if it remains unpublished, or until 2027 if the work is published before 2002.

Work of Art	*Duration*
1. Created in 1978 or later	Life of the artist plus 50 years
2. First Copyright term (28 years) in effect as of January 1, 1978	Renewal term for additional 47 years
3. Second Copyright term (28 years) in effect as of January 1, 1978	Automatic extension of additional 19 years
4. Created before 1978 but not published as of January 1, 1978	Life of the artist plus 50 years. If artist died 50 or more years prior to January 1, 1978 1) copyright until 2002 if work remains unpublished, or 2) copyright until 2027 if the work is published before 2002.

Calculation of duration may seem somewhat complicated, but it is vitally important for an artist to know the extent to which his or her exclusive rights in a work are protected against infringement. From a commercial point of view, this knowledge is particularly important for an artist who is deriving ongoing income from copyrighted works. Many currently active artists will continue to be affected by the 1909 and 1976 Acts for their lifetimes because they have produced works before and after 1978.

OWNERSHIP OF COPYRIGHT

Generally, with some exceptions, a copyright belongs to the creator or creators of an original work of authorship. This includes a painter, sculptor, author, choreographer, or anyone else who creates a copyrightable work. For artists, the most important exception to this rule is the "work made for hire" concept.

The term "work made for hire" arises in two categories of situations: where a work is created for an employer and where a work is commissioned. Where a work of art (or any other copyrightable work) is designated a "work made for hire" the copyright does not belong to the artist. It belongs to the employer or the commissioning party. But not all works created as commissions or in the employment relationship are "works made for hire." Artists should pay close attention to the following definitions because many of you produce most of your work in relationships that could result in "works made for hire."

A "work made for hire" in an employment situation is one produced within the scope of the artist's employment, that is, at the direction and expense of the employer. Generally, if the work produced is part of your job, it is a "work made for hire." But what if your job description has little or no relation to the work of art produced for the employer? Whether yours is a "work made for hire" will be determined by the facts of the situation. If the employer has no right to control or direct the artwork, you may own the copyright as the author of the work. For example, you have a job as an ice cream jockey at a dessert parlor and your boss learns of your skill as an artist. He asks you to prepare a new logo and artwork for the menus and offers to pay you extra for the work. If your employer has only a right of approval of your final work but does not control the content, the artwork you produce is probably not a "work made for hire." Thus, you are likely to be considered the copyright owner. Other situations can be rather close calls. However, where it is fairly clear-cut that the work is produced as part of your normal job, the employer is presumed under the law to be the author for copyright purposes unless you enter into a written contract with the employer agreeing to the contrary. Whether an employer is willing to enter into such an agreement will usually depend upon your bargaining power and the economic consequences to the employer. Even where you are confident that the work you create for your employer does not fall within the duties of your employment, you should protect yourself with some form of written agreement signed by the employer stating that you, the employee, own the copyright to the work.

Where a work is commissioned, there are only nine circumstances in which such work is potentially eligible to be called a "work made for hire." These are where the work is created for use as: a contribution to a collective work, a part of a motion picture or other audiovisual work, a translation, a supplementary work, a compilation, an instructional text, a test, answer material for a test, or an atlas. However, even where the work in question falls into one of these categories, the work is not a "work made for hire" unless the parties expressly so agree in writing.

Where you are commissioned to do a work that does not arguably fall within one of the nine circumstances listed above, the work is clearly not a "work made for hire" because the federal copyright law will not permit such a work to be a "work made for hire." For example, you are commissioned to paint a person's portrait. Upon its creation, you, the artist, own the copyright. The only way the patron can become the copyright owner is if you assign the copyright to that person. In a "work made for hire" situation, the commissioning party is the copyright owner from the very beginning. The artist assigns nothing because the artist does not own the copyright in a "work made for hire." In the context of an ordinary commission, the artist, as copyright owner, may do with his copyright as he pleases, including assigning it to the commissioning party. With an assignment, the assignee will likely seek to record the assignment with the Copyright Office to ensure that the author or artist does not later grant the same right to someone else who might then record the assignment ahead of the first assignee. In the case of two such assignments, with the exception of a brief grace period for the first assignee, the first to be recorded is the valid one.

The duration of the copyright of a "work made for hire" is different from that of other works. The copyright lasts for 100 years from creation or 75 years from publication, whichever is shorter. This issue, however, is of little interest to the creator of the work because, unlike ordinary transfers of an artist's copyright, the creator of the work has no right to terminate the copyright interest of the owner of a "work made for hire" after a certain number of years. (See discussion under "Transfer of Exclusive Rights" below). This is because the artist is not considered to be the legal owner of the copyright to begin with.

It is important to note that with works produced prior to 1978, the old law was much less favorable to the creators of copyrightable works. The law presumed that in the commission context, the copyright is owned by the commissioning party. This is another example of where the new copyright law is more favorable to artists.

Some artists frequently contribute to larger works consisting of a collection of various artists' or authors' efforts. The current copyright law also provides copyright protection for such collective works or compilations, such as newspapers, periodicals, calendars, anthologies, art catalogues, or other collections of various copyrightable works. Often, such works will contain some original material produced by the author of the collective work and a great deal more of work from pre-existing sources, such as photographs, engravings, or various types of illustrations of works of art. As an example, let's look at a book on the history of candid photography. This work will contain written contributions by other authors as well as text by the author of the book. The bulk of the book, however, will consist of pre-existing photographs by numerous photographers.

The author of the book is entitled to a copyright on the work as a whole. Of course, permission must be obtained from the copyright owners of the pre-existing works if any of those works have valid copyrights. The copyright law permits a single copyright notice for the collective work to cover all separate contributions. Let's assume the copyright notice for the photography book is in the name of Tiny LaGrande, the author. Even though the book may contain copyrighted photos by a hundred different photographers, each of these copyrights remains valid under Tiny LaGrande's notice. However, there is nothing wrong legally with including a separate notice for each individual contribution. The single indispensable precaution that you, the artist, must take where your work will be included in a collective work is to state in writing that your authorization to allow your copyrighted work to be used is conditioned on the requirement that the collective work contain a copyright notice. If you have the bargaining power, you might even be able to require that a separate notice in your name be included with your contribution.

If you have contributed a photograph to Tiny's book, what can he do with your photo? Assuming you own the copyright to your photograph, he can do nothing other than what you have authorized. (Incidentally, Tiny presumably has paid you a fee for the use of your work.) He may continue to reproduce the collective work, but he has no right to reproduce your photo by itself or to use your photo in another book or other work. Tiny LaGrande will only have exclusive rights in the materials he himself has authored and in the organization of the book. If he wants to own the exclusive rights to the entire contents of the book, he would have to obtain a transfer of the copyright from each individual contributor.

For artists who are not U.S. citizens, entitlement to and ownership of copyright can be a more complicated matter. For such people, there are statutory guidelines under the 1976 Copyright Act to determine whether or not copyright protection will be accorded to their works. As long as the work of a foreign artist is unpublished, copyright protection exists for that work in the United States. Once publication occurs anywhere in the world, copyright protection depends upon whether the artist belongs to one of several classes of individuals. If the foreign artist has his or her domicile in the United States, or if the work is first published in the United States regardless of the nationality or domicile of the artist, the artwork is eligible for copyright. If the artist is a national of, or has his or her domicile in, a nation that has a copyright treaty with the United States or if the work is published in a nation that belongs to the Universal Copyright Convention, the artwork is also eligible for copyright. The final method by which a foreign artist may obtain copyright protection is by presidential proclamation. The President has the authority to extend copyright eligibility to nationals of countries where the President believes Americans are given equal treatment under the other nation's copyright law.

The Universal Copyright Convention is by far the most important copyright treaty to which the United States belongs. This treaty provides copyright protection in other member nations for works by U.S. nationals or domiciliaries as well as protection in the United States for foreign artists and authors. The sole requirement to obtain the maximum benefit of the Universal Copyright Convention is to affix a copyright notice in the form of the "c" -in-the-circle, year of first publication and name of the work's maker.

If a foreign artist is not able to qualify for one of the methods of eligibility for copyright protection in the United States, his or her works will be considered to be in the public domain. The result is that anyone may copy such work.

The United States is not yet a member of the Berne Convention, an intellectual property treaty to which most other major nations belong. The Berne Convention grants significantly greater protection to artists and authors than does the Universal Copyright Convention or United States law. However, an American can obtain international copyright protection by means of the Berne Convention in two ways: first, if the work is published in a Berne Convention nation within thirty days of first publication in the United States, or second, if first publication of the American's work is made in a Berne Convention nation and the author has complied with the publication laws of that country. (See page 108 for a partial list of signatories to the Convention. Be aware that the scope of the Berne Convention rights are not identical among all nations belonging to the Convention.)

TRANSFERS OF THE EXCLUSIVE RIGHTS

Since the exclusive rights are the property of the copyright owner, that owner may transfer his or her exclusive rights in the same manner as he or she would any other kind of property. The rights may be individually sold, leased, licensed or given away. Moreover, individual rights can be transferred to more than one person at a time as long as the transfer is not exclusive. For example, you can grant a non-exclusive license for reproduction of a work to any number of people. Or you can grant exclusive licenses on a geographic basis to more than one party. Although it may be more common to transfer at one time the entire bundle of exclusive rights under the copyright, the artist should at least be aware of the potential for dealing with the exclusive rights separately. (For example, you could grant United States rights for the area east of the Mississippi to one person and west of the Mississippi to another, or North American rights to one person, French rights to another, and so on.)

Keep in mind that an artist's rights in the physical work of art are distinct from the exclusive rights. Thus, an artist who creates a work may transfer some or all of the exclusive rights at the same time he or she transfers ownership of the physical object. The artist may also retain ownership of the work of art but separately transfer interests in the exclusive rights.

Any transfer of copyright ownership, except the grant of a non-exclusive license, must be in writing in order to be valid. The copyright office will also record any type of transfer of copyright ownership and provide a certificate of recordation for a fee. While this service may be of little importance to many artists, proof of recordation by someone to whom an artist transfers copyright ownership could be crucial in the event of a later dispute about copyright ownership.

TERMINATION

The 1976 Act provides for the automatic right of an artist or author to terminate any interest he or she has conveyed in a copyright after a minimum of thirty-five years (but no more than forty years) have passed since the execution of the transfer. This provision in the law gives an artist (or his survivors) a second opportunity to control the copyright in his own works. An artist's right to terminate a transfer of copyright cannot be waived in advance or be contracted away. But this right only applies to works produced after January 1, 1978.

The termination can take effect any time during a five-year period which begins at the end of thirty-five years from the date of execution of the transfer of interest in the copyright. However, if the transfer was for the right of publication, the five-year period begins at the end of thirty-five years from the date of publication of the work or at the end of forty years from the date of execution, whichever is earlier. You must give written notice to the transferee informing that person when you intend to terminate the transfer. That notice cannot be given more than ten years before the intended date of termination, nor less than two years prior. You must also record the notice in the Copyright Office. The Register of Copyrights prescribes the form of the notice. In the event you decide to exercise this right, you should contact the Copyright Office for current forms.

INFRINGEMENT

Despite your best efforts to avoid legal problems, there might come a time when one of your copyrights is violated. After attempting an informal approach to solving the problem, you might require the intervention of a lawyer to go any further with the matter. You will then be faced with the possibility of suing the copyright infringer. Although the details of lawsuits take us beyond the scope of this book, it is important that you have a general idea of what a copyright plaintiff in a lawsuit must prove in order to prevail. This information is also useful in providing you with some general guidelines to avoid becoming a copyright infringer yourself.

The violation of any one of the exclusive rights constitutes copyright infringement. Frequently, however, individual exclusive rights overlap. As a result, an infringement of a copyrighted work can include violations of more than one of the enumerated rights. In fact, anyone in the commercial chain can be liable for copyright infringement, from the copier to the distributor to a person who displays the work.

In order to establish a copyright infringment, the plaintiff must prove both that he owns the copyright and that unauthorized copying occurred. Since direct evidence of copying may be difficult to come by, the plaintiff may prove infringement by showing that the defendant had access to the copyrighted work and that the allegedly infringing work is "substantially similar" to the copyrighted work. "Substantial similarity" is not a precise term, but artists, publishers, manufacturers and others must keep this standard in mind in order to determine the point at which they may be subject to a lawsuit for copyright infringement. This is not to say that one artist cannot be inspired by the work of another. In fact, the subject matter of an artist's work cannot be copyrighted. For example, suppose Guido, the painter, produces a portrait of Ricardo Bundingi, a famous choral director, and the portrait becomes extremely well known and commercially valuable. If another artist, let's call him William Rainmaker Henchman, produces a portrait of Mr. Bundingi without copying from Guido's work, the second work is also entitled to copyright protection even if there is similarity between the works. Of course, the more similarity there is between works by two individuals, the greater the suspicion that the later work copied or borrowed elements from the earlier one.

If Mr. Henchman produces a portrait of Mr. Bundingi that uses a quality of light, as well as a palette of color and brushstrokes similar to those in Guido's portrait, a jury might find that he has stepped into the forbidden zone. The determination of whether an infringement occurred is a fact issue that is determined by the jury. Important information in Mr. Henchman's case would be the past work of the artist. Do his earlier works show close stylistic and technical affinities with his portrait of Mr. Bundingi? If not, a fairly strong case for infringement can probably be made, particularly if Mr. Bundingi did not sit for the artist. There is no bright line separating infringements from lawful similarities. But it is important to know that even copying from memory might constitute infringement. The jury will be looking at two works of art, one by the plaintiff and the other by the defendant. If they find more similarity between the works than one can reasonably expect mere chance to produce, they are likely to find "substantial similarity." Assuming access to the copyrighted work is shown, the jury will very likely conclude that an infringement occurred.

Because copyright is a form of property which the artist can transfer to another party, it is even possible for the creator of a work of art to infringe the copyright on that very work by producing a later work that is substantially similar to the earlier one. This would be true whether or not the artist continued to own the first work of art. As long as the artist transferred his copyright to another party, he is precluded from infringing that copyright just as any other artist would be. Again, whether substantial similarity exists is a question of fact. However, a jury could not reasonably find that a later work by the same artist was substantially similar to one of his earlier works merely because there is some stylistic similarity between the two. To conclude otherwise would be to penalize an artist for developing a distinctive style.

If you win a copyright infringement case, you are entitled to recover your actual damages caused by the infringement as well as the infringer's profits to the extent they are not figured into your actual damages calculation. There's even a bonus if you registered your work within three months of first publication. Under those circumstances, you are also entitled to recover your attorneys' fees and statutory damages in lieu of proving your actual damages. The statutory damages awarded will be no less than $250 nor more than $5000. However, where intentional infringement is proved, statutory damages can be as high as $50,000.

Producing original artwork in the style of other artists can raise other potential problems besides copyright. If a work, albeit original, is passed off as the work of another artist, the person who misrepresents the identity of the artist is subject to legal action on a variety of grounds, both civil and criminal. Possible plaintiffs include buyers of the art, the artist whose name is wrongfully attributed to the work, dealers or other retailers, and state and federal governments.

COPYRIGHT PRECAUTIONS

The following is a summary of the simple precautions you can take to avoid most of the problems connected with copyright. They won't necessarily stop a willful infringer, but they will put you in a better position in the unfortunate event that you have to bring a lawsuit to protect one of your copyrights.

1. Affix a copyright notice to your artwork no later than the time the work is complete. Works-in-progress are entitled to copyright protection. Remember, it is not necessary to deface or alter your work to affix a proper copyright notice.

2. Register your copyright. The current fee is $10 per copyright. Registration within five years of publication is mandatory where the copyrighted work has been "published" without notice of copyright and the number of copies distributed is more than a handful. The alternative is dedication of the work to the public domain. Registration is a pre-requisite for bringing an infringement lawsuit. Registration within three months of "publication" permits the plaintiff to recover attorney's fees and statutory damages.

3. Contracts for reproductions of your work in any medium and in any form should be in writing and should include the requirement that a legally effective copyright notice appear with the reproduction. (The same applies to any textual material.)

4. Do not incorporate the work of another artist into your own work unless you know the work is in the public domain or written permission has been received from the copyright owner.

2

WRITTEN AGREEMENTS

Skeezix D. is a metal sculptor who has been working at his art for fifteen years and making a living from it for the last five. Six months ago, a mutual friend introduced Skeezix to a wealthy real estate developer. The developer was quite taken by Skeezix' sculpture and asked if he would be interested in creating a large wall piece on commission. The developer had in mind a detailed rendering of a group of Victorian period houses. Skeezix was intrigued with the project and was in need of the substantial fee he could expect from the undertaking. He expressed his interest and suggested that he produce some drawings for review by the developer.

Two weeks later, Skeezix presented several designs, one of which the developer approved. At the same time, the developer gave the go-ahead for the project. Skeezix then asked for a $1000 materials advance. The developer offered $600 to start, but agreed to review the situation after he saw some results. Skeezix took the $600 reluctantly, but accepted because the commission would be of great help in furthering his career.

Skeezix promptly began working. He soon realized, however, that this was a major undertaking which would require four or five months. At the next meeting between artist and patron, Skeezix informed the developer that the piece would take more time and thus be more expensive than he had originally thought. Skeezix asked the developer if he wanted to put a specific limit on the cost of the piece. The developer assured him that he admired Skeezix' work sufficiently that the cost was not important. "Proceed with the project," he said, "and do your best work." He then gave Skeezix another $400 for materials.

Did Skeezix and the developer have a contract at this point? They certainly had nothing in writing; there was no agreement as to price. However, there did seem to be some agreement with respect to what the final sculpture would be. The work continued and the developer visited the studio on two subsequent occasions, expressing his approval of the work, and encouraging the artist to continue. At the time of the developer's last visit, Skeezix had been at work for five weeks and had already cut and assembled 1500 pieces of metal.

After two months, Skeezix became concerned because he and the developer had no firm agreement on price. He telephoned the developer to obtain a commitment to be paid. The developer said he was still interested but could not agree on a price until he saw the final work. Skeezix objected and insisted that that was not their agreement. The developer said he had not agreed to anything specific but that, in any event, he would pay what was fair. Besides, he assured Skeezix, with $1000 invested in materials, he had no incentive to refuse the piece.

Skeezix was not in a strong position. He had put in two months of work, the sculpture was over half completed, with 2000 pieces already cut and assembled. If he quit now, he would have wasted a great deal of time. If he completed the sculpture, however, and the developer then refused to pay for it, the piece would be quite difficult to sell because of its size. By working intensely for another month, Skeezix completed the work. The wall sculpture was twelve feet long by four feet high and consisted of approximately 4000 individual pieces.

The developer came to Skeezix' studio to see the completed work. When Skeezix broached the subject of payment, the developer offered a sum which Skeezix considered an insult. When Skeezix quoted what he believed to be a fair price, the developer expressed shock and said that he could buy a museum piece for that amount. In addition, he complained that the work was heavier than he had expected, and thus would cost considerably more to mount.

Since Skeezix realized he was in a weak bargaining position, he lowered his price slightly. The developer refused to pay that amount, too. They were at loggerheads. After some further sparring, the developer left the studio, informing Skeezix that when he, Skeezix, was willing to be reasonable, they would arrive at a mutually satisfactory price.

Skeezix attempted to reach the developer on numerous subsequent occasions without success. Skeezix eventually retained a lawyer and sued the developer. Skeezix demanded $20,000 in his lawsuit. The developer offered $3,000 to settle. Although his lawyer encouraged him to hold out for substantially more money, Skeezix was so demoralized that he accepted the $3,000 offer just to put the ordeal behind him. Today, the developer proudly shows off his "bargain" work of art.

Could Skeezix have avoided a lawsuit for payment? Possibly not. But the existence of a written contract (plus a firm demand for a more substantial advance) would have dissuaded the developer from casually denying the existence of an agreement, or risking the loss of his front money. But what kind of contract would have helped Skeezix? After reading this chapter, you should be able to offer him your own advice.

THE NATURE OF CONTRACTS

An agreement between two or more parties to do or refrain from doing something is a contract, so long as there is consideration for the agreement. "Consideration" is a somewhat vague legal term meaning that each party both gives up something and gains something in the bargain. For example, if Guido the painter volunteers to paint his neighbor's garage as a courtesy and fails to carry through, no contract was made and the neighbor cannot enforce Guido's promise in court. There was no consideration for Guido's promise.

Contracts can be oral or written. Both are enforceable in a court of law (with some exceptions regarding oral contracts as discussed below). Yet, written contracts have advantages over oral ones. Precision of terms and protection against fraud or conflicting memories of what was agreed upon are the primary benefits of a written contract. If it becomes necessary to consider suing on a contract, the proof will generally be much simpler with a written contract.

A written contract is a document or a series of documents reciting the material terms of the agreement and signed by the party or parties to be charged (or their agents) with the contractual obligations. Such material terms usually include price, time for performance of the obligations, the scope of the work or description of the merchandise, and any other conditions without which either of the parties would not have agreed to go forward with the deal. A contract is most often created when one party makes an offer which the other party accepts. Counteroffers may be exchanged, but the last act is the acceptance. There is no limit to the number of parties, but there must be at least two live human beings or business entities legally competent to enter into the agreement at the time it is formed.

There is no such thing as a standard contract. The parties or their lawyers generally trade a draft of an agreement back and forth, each side editing the document to satisfy its own needs, until the contract language is mutually acceptable. Often one party offers its usual agreement to the other and that forms a starting point for the negotiations. The party with the greater bargaining power (the party who can most easily forego the agreement) usually prepares the first draft and usually prevails in the negotiations.

In order for a court to enforce an agreement, there must be a valid contract. While probably most oral contracts are valid, it is advisable and in some cases necessary that it be in writing. The statute of frauds (a version of which is the law in every state) generally requires that any contract for the sale of real estate or a contract in which one person agrees to answer for the debts of another, or a contract which is not capable of being performed within one year be in writing. The Uniform Commercial Code (which applies in every state except Louisiana) requires that contracts for the sale of goods costing $500 or more be in writing. Complex contracts should always be in writing, and amendments to written agreements must generally be in writing.

As an example, an artist who consigns three of his paintings to a dealer for sale for a period not to exceed three months is not legally required by the statute of frauds to commit the agreement to writing in order to enforce it. In the event of a dispute over precisely what the obligations of the parties are, however, it is highly desirable to have a written contract for reference to determine what the parties decided at the outset.

If the artist is consigning his works to a gallery for exhibition and sale, the basic terms to be covered are as follows:

1. Precisely which objects are to be consigned (title, medium, size).

2. The prices of the objects and the commission to be paid to the dealer (a certain percentage of the sale price or a certain amount on sale).

3. The duration of the contract (also referred to as the term of the contract).

4. Who is responsible for loss, damage and cost of insurance.

5. Who is responsible for framing and framing costs.

6. Who is responsible for shipping and shipping costs.

7. Who is responsible for photographic reproductions and publicity costs (including costs of receptions).

8. What special restrictions, if any, will be placed on the sale (e.g., artist unwilling to transfer copyright, artist's approval of installation, etc.).

9. Whether resale royalties will be paid to the artist (required by statute in California).

10. Whether the object may be loaned to any other party, and, if so, what restrictions apply.

11. The disposition of unsold works.

12. Whether the dealer is the artist's agent and/or fiduciary (required by statute in some states).

13. The time and method of payment to the artist.

14. The artist's warranties that the objects are not encumbered by liens and that the objects are original.

15. Disclosures of special information about multiples (required by statute in some states) for example, whether the edition is limited and, if so, how large it is.

16. The number and type of exhibitions the dealer will hold.

17. Whether the agreement is assignable.

18. Whether the agreement will survive the death of the artist (i.e., applies to the estate of the artist).

19. Possible arbitration or mediation for disputes.

See the Appendix for a sample agreement between a dealer and an artist.

Well drafted contracts state a term of duration, and many provide the basis upon which either party may terminate the contract by providing a specific period of advance notice to the other party. If the agreement is silent about its duration, it may continue indefinitely until one of the parties breaches the contract or ceases to exist (such as when an individual dies or a business ceases operation with no successor taking over), or until the contract no longer has any purpose or until all the terms have been met. For example, a consignment contract between an artist and dealer has been fully satisfied when all the objects are sold. If, however, the contract is for "all" of the artist's works (a so-called output contract), it may continue until the artist dies.

If the dealer sells the gallery to another party, he may; unless the contract forbids it, usually assign his rights and delegate his duties under the contract to that other party. If the contract between the artist and gallery expressly so provides, a consignment agreement between the parties may survive the death of the artist. This means that the relationship that existed between the artist and gallery will continue between the gallery and the artist's estate. This may be very important where the estate must quickly raise funds to pay estate taxes or where market demand for the artist's work is high at the time of death. Where a separate agreement must be reached between gallery and estate, many months may pass before the deceased artist's works are made available for sale. This situation could have a considerably adverse effect upon the artist's heirs.

An artist should definitely obtain a written agreement from any museum which borrows his work. In fact, the museum will probably offer the artist its standard loan agreement to sign. Such a contract should include many of the terms outlined above for consignment agreements. Other special provisions particularly necessary in museum loan agreements, some of which are governed by state statutes, are as follows:

1. The artist's responsibility to keep the museum advised of his mailing address.

2. The consequences of failure by the artist to claim the object after a specified period of time.

3. Whether the museum has permission to reproduce the object in a catalogue.

4. Whether the museum has permission to sell reproductions of the object.

5. Whether the museum has permission to restore the object, if necessary, and whether the artist must be consulted in that case.

6. How and where the object will be displayed.

7. What the label will say, (for example, whether the loan will be advertised as anonymous).

8. Whether the object may travel to other museums

9. Whether the museum will provide legal counsel to the artist in the event he is sued in connection with the exhibit and will indemnify the artist for any money judgment obtained against him.

10. The appraised value of the object.

At least one state (California) has a statute governing long-term or indefinite loans to museums. It is important for artists or anyone else contemplating such loans to be aware of state laws that might have an effect upon the rights of the object's owner. Legislation in the various states relating to the visual arts increases yearly. It is therefore very likely that other states will adopt laws affecting loans to museums.

Contracts are especially important for commissioned artworks, whether the commissioning party is private or public. Artwork for public places, which is becoming a requirement for public and private developers of real property, should be commissioned by written contract only. In such situations, an artist may be asked to sign two contracts—one for a model to be considered by a committee and another in case the model is selected as the winner. The artist contemplating a commission for a public location will be entering into an agreement in which many parties are affected. If the space is a large one, the artwork and the architecture may well have to be planned together, with the consulting advice of more than one architect, landscape architect, engineer and public planner. It is therefore essential that the performance obligations of the artist be specified as clearly as possible in the contract. It should include the following, in addition to the basic points listed above:

1. Payment schedule for partial payment as the work is completed.
2. Whether the object is a "work made for hire" under the copyright law.
3. Whether the artist or patron owns the models
4. Who owns the copyright.
5. Whether the artist must participate in publicity events.
6. Who will install the work.
7. The artist's warranty that the work is safe for the public.
8. A clear description of the climate to which the work will be exposed and the expected frequency of maintenance.
9. Whether the artist or patron is responsible for maintenance.
10. Whether the patron will be responsible to the artist for third-party acts, such as vandalism.
11. Precisely where the object will be exhibited.
12. Whether the artist may sell other works similar to or inspired by this one.
13. Whether the artist must be consulted about repairs or removal (some states, including California, have statutes requiring such conduct).
14. Whether the artist will be given extensions of time for inability to meet the completion deadline.
15. The artist's remedy if the work is rejected by the patron at delivery.
16. Whether the patron may sell the site to a buyer who may use the property for an unrelated purpose.

See the Appendix for an example of a city contract with an artist for a commission.

Depending upon the nature of the agreement and the nature of the artist's problem, a wide variety of results may follow the situation in which an artist fails for some reason to live up to his commitments in a contract. A few basic cases follow.

If the artist is somehow incapacitated or if in some way his performance under the contract is actually impossible, he will be excused. For example, if Guido the painter is commissioned to paint a portrait but he is hospitalized involuntarily or if the sitter refuses to cooperate, Guido will be excused from painting the portrait. If, on the other hand, Guido decides to have a purely elective face-lift and is hospitalized during the time he is supposed to be painting, he will not be excused from performing under the contract. Of course, this is a two-way street: If an artist is commissioned to paint a mural for a specific building and a terrorist blows up the building, the patron will generally be excused from performing his obligations under the contract.

Where it becomes impossible for an artist to perform and the situation is only temporary, through no fault of his own, the artist is not obligated to perform under the contract. However, he is not discharged from his obligations under the contract unless they would be substantially greater after the impossibility ceases, If, for example, an artist recovers from an illness and is faced with other contractual obligations that only become due after the illness, the artist should be permanently excused from producing the commissioned portrait mentioned above. Where the artist would be able to carry out the commission after becoming well again, with no other serious conflicts, the contract would probably be enforceable against him.

In situations where the artist cannot be excused on the grounds of impossibility of performance, his failure to perform will be called a breach, and a court may require the artist to pay the other party money damages. If the contract recites that a fixed amount must be paid as liquidated damages, that amount will usually suffice. Where the contract calls for arbitration of a dispute, that remedy will usually be exclusive and the arbitrator will determine what, if anything, the artist must do or pay.

Similarly, if the non-artist breaches the contract, the artist may sue the other party to collect the amount due and possibly to compel specific performance of the contract where that is the only fair remedy. Specific performance is a remedy compelling the breaching party to carry out his end of the bargain. It is used most often where the obligation is to perform some action for which a money payment is not an adequate substitute. For example, if Guido and Skeezix agree to exchange houses, and Guido receives the deed to Skeezix' house but refuses to give up his own, a court might well award specific performance as Skeezix' remedy because the subject of the contract—the real property—is unique and money damages would not be adequate.

Generally, a court will not require specific performance where a breach is caused by a party who contracts to provide personal services. The artist who breaches a contract to paint a portrait is not likely to be ordered to paint the portrait against his will. A money judgment will probably suffice. Where an artist has contracted to sell or consign an existing work of art, however, a court is much more likely to require specific performance from the artist.

In any event, when a defendant loses a lawsuit over a contract, the court does not impose an extra penalty on that party. (Contrast a lawsuit over a tort where a losing defendant might have to pay punitive damages in addition to actual damages.) If specific performance is not required, a money judgment will be awarded in favor of the winning party. Generally speaking, the purpose of a money judgment is to give the winner the benefit of the deal. This is measured in numerous ways. Where profits were expected as part of the contract and such profits can be reasonably calculated, the court will award lost profits to the winner. Sometimes the winner will receive the amount of money he had expended in reliance on the contract being performed by the other party.

Some contracts contain a liquidated damages provision. In the event of breach, this provision states the amount of money the breaching party must pay to the non-breaching party. Liquidated damages are recognized by courts, but only where the amount in question is reasonably related to the terms of the agreement. If the amount in question is disproportionately large, courts will reject liquidated damages clauses on the ground that they are really penalties and not substitutes for ordinary contract damages.

Many of the documents an artist works with are contracts to at least some degree. Leases, discussed below in Chapter 5, are in part contracts between landlord and tenant. Purchase orders for supplies are contracts, the terms of which usually appear on the seller's order form in what is commonly referred to as boilerplate. In all of the agreements, the money or performance paid by one side to the other is the consideration. Without the obligation of consideration, a mere gratuitous promise is not enforceable in court.

On the other hand, contractual obligations can arise quite casually. When one party has created the expectation of performance such that the other party relies on it to his own detriment, a contract may be formed. For example, Skeezix the sculptor promises to deliver one of his garden sculptures to the home of a patron in time for the opening of the patron's new courtyard. In reliance on the arrival of Skeezix' work, the patron has placed an expensive marble base in the courtyard for the sculpture, and has purchased food and drink for one hundred guests whom he has invited to the opening. The expenses for the base and the party total $1500, the amount which the patron may be said to have spent in reliance on that sculpture being delivered to him. If Skeezix refuses to deliver, the patron may sue him to force him to deliver the sculpture even though no money has changed hands between them, or to collect $1500, the amount the patron has spent in expectation that the sculpture would be delivered.

Even though contracts can be made casually, they require the intent to make an agreement. For this reason, it is especially desirable to prepare written contracts which are generally considered evidence of that intent once the parties sign them. An artist may rely to his detriment on an oral promise from a friend to buy his painting foregoing the opportunity to sell the painting to someone else. When the friend refuses to fulfill his promise and the artist sues him for his lost opportunity to sell to the second buyer or to force the friend to buy the painting, the artist may lose the case if the friend proves he never actually intended to enter into an agreement to buy the painting. He was just puffing. The friend might produce evidence that he and the artist were clearly drunk when the alleged deal was made, or that the friend had just declared bankruptcy and the artist knew he had no money with which to buy any artwork.

Written contracts should be thought of as protection. Without such armor, the artist should venture into the marketplace very cautiously. When signing a written offer prepared by the other party, an artist should read carefully and discuss any provisions with which he is not comfortable with someone else. Consulting a lawyer before signing and thereby creating a contract may well be worth the time and money.

3

THE ARTIST-DEALER RELATIONSHIP

Jimmy Barswell was a student at a midwestern university where he majored in art. His talent as a sculptor was already obvious in his sophomore year. By the time he was a senior, Jimmy was well known locally. His works were exhibited in a local gallery and were shown regularly in student art exhibitions. In the months before graduation, Jimmy had three works in a well publicized student show. Among those attending the exhibition was an alumnus of the university, a highly successful but less than fully reputable art dealer from Phoenix. Let's call him H.E. Robsham.

Mr. Robsham had a good eye and could recognize talent. He was confident there was a market for Jimmy's work in Phoenix and other parts of the Southwest. Robsham introduced himself and made an offer to represent Jimmy through the H.E. Robsham gallery. He also invited Jimmy to visit him in Phoenix, all expenses paid. This was the break Jimmy was looking for. Even though he had never heard of Mr. Robsham there didn't seem to be much risk in pursuing the offer. After all, Robsham was articulate, immaculately dressed and had invited Jimmy to Phoenix to become better acquainted and to visit the gallery.

Jimmy accepted the invitation, and had a glorious time in Phoenix. At the end of his visit, Jimmy accepted Robsham's offer to represent him. Unfortunately for Jimmy, the arrangement was completed with nothing more than a handshake. When Jimmy asked whether they shouldn't have something in writing, Robsham became incensed. His relationship with his artists, he said, is like that of a father and son. The relationship is based on mutual respect and trust. If Jimmy required a piece of paper for reassurance, then it would be clear that the necessary trust did not exist between them.

In due course, Jimmy had enough sculpture to support his first one-person show; it was a sell-out. But when it came time to account for Jimmy's share of the proceeds there were some rude surprises. First, the gallery declared its commission for new artists to be 65% of retail. Second, half of all reproduction and printing costs, half of all costs of the opening reception, and half of all shipping and insurance costs were charged against the artist's account.

In fact, the accounting wasn't provided to Jimmy until four months after the exhibition was over, and only after Jimmy made repeated requests for it. H.E. Robsham was never available on the telephone. He finally informed Jimmy by letter of the total proceeds and the various charges against his account. Jimmy protested that this was inconsistent with the 40% commission that Robsham said he ordinarily charged for sales of his artists' works. Robsham responded that Jimmy was being treated fairly according to Robsham's customary arrangements with new artists. Robsham explained that the risk a gallery takes with a new artist is much greater than the risk assumed by the artist.

It was six months before Jimmy was paid. Various excuses were offered, and finally Jimmy informed Robsham by letter that he, Jimmy, was terminating the relationship with the gallery. Robsham responded with cajolery, reminding Jimmy of the benefit to his reputation as an artist that Robsham Galleries had provided with the success of his first show. He also reminded Jimmy of the expense involved in launching public interest in a new artist's career, and that to recoup his expenses he would need at least another major show of Jimmy's work. When Jimmy refused to do another exhibition, Robsham irately informed Jimmy that if he were so ungrateful and insensitive to the business aspects of running a gallery, Robsham will have no choice but to bring legal action against him.

The threat worked. Jimmy was concerned about possible damage to his reputation by an angry gallery owner and also feared being sued. So Jimmy did another show. Once again, the show sold out despite the fact that Robsham had raised prices substantially. This time Jimmy waited eight months before being paid. In the interim, realizing that he could never make a living in this manner, he sought some legal and business advice. The result was that Jimmy turned the tables on the dealer. In his final letter to H.E. Robsham, Jimmy made a demand for payment for the amount owed him plus interest. He included in the letter the list of charges against his account he considered to be arbitrary and unacceptable, stated that the two parties had never agreed to terms apart from those Jimmy was coerced into accepting, announced that the relationship was terminated and that he, Jimmy, would sue Robsham unless the account was paid up within thirty days.

A check was delivered to Jimmy on the 30th day. Enclosed with it was a note of outrage from H.E. Robsham who announced that Jimmy's career was finished in the southwest.

This story may not be typical of new artists, but it does illustrate the need to have a clearly defined agreement with a dealer before you allow him to represent you. Your expectations and those of the dealer should be based on a clear understanding between the parties. The terms of an agreement can vary greatly from one artist-dealer relationship to another; whatever terms you ultimately agree upon, put the agreement in writing. It does not have to be a formal contract, although that is generally preferable. A letter of agreement will suffice. The important thing is that all major terms be expressed.

Although many artists have had satisfactory relationships with dealers based on a handshake, you cannot assume that you will be so fortunate. A dealer who expresses a dislike for written agreements may be giving you an important message regarding his or her abilities and trustworthiness as a businessperson.

For the actual subject areas you might consider for inclusion in an artist-dealer contract, see Chapter 2. The list provided there probably contains far more items than you are likely to need in your agreement, but you should at least review the list to determine which matters are appropriate to your situation. Even if you are not in a strong bargaining position with a dealer, you may still decide that the terms offered by the dealer are too one-sided and, as a result, prefer to look elsewhere.

An important matter to resolve with your dealer at the beginning of the relationship is whether you as the artist are permitted to sell your work directly to a third party without paying a commission to your dealer. Some dealers insist upon having the exclusive power to sell an artist's works. This means that they are entitled to their commission any time one of the artist's works is sold, even if the dealer does not do the selling. If you, the artist, sell a piece out of your studio, your dealer might demand his commission on that sale. Even where you did not realize any cash proceeds from a transaction, such as when you trade art for services, your dealer could demand a cash commission.

If you feel strongly about your ability to remain independent and free to sell works not consigned to the dealer, clarify this matter with your dealer before you sign a contract. If the matter has never been discussed and you are already in a relationship with a dealer, you have a strong argument that your dealer does not have an exclusive power to sell, since it is reasonable to assume that an exclusive power to sell would be a major aspect of an artist-dealer representation agreement. If your written or oral agreement does not contain such a term, then the exclusive power to sell could not reasonably be considered part of that agreement. But this only means that you can sell or otherwise transfer ownership in your own work. The dealer may still have an exclusive *agency* for the sale of your art. That depends upon the terms of your contract or agreement—if you have given an exclusive agency to someone to represent you as an artist, you may not engage anyone else to represent you or sell your work for you without breaching your agreement. Often the exclusive agency is limited by geographical area. For example, if an artist's New York dealer has an exclusive agency for any sales made east of the Mississippi, it would not be a breach of the agreement for the artist to grant an exclusive agency to a California dealer for sales made west of the Mississippi.

Some dealers may not have thought about whether the artists they represent should be able to sell their work directly during the term of the contract. You, as the artist, may not be inclined to raise the issue out of concern that you might alert the dealer to what would otherwise not be a problem. One way of approaching the issue is to clarify that the dealer's agency extends only to the works that you consign to the dealer. This way the dealer has no grounds for claiming that he has been denied his rightful commission. Even though as a practical matter a dealer may not be able to police private sales by the artist, the artist-dealer relationship will be a much healthier one if both parties are candid with one another.

THE NATURE OF THE ARTIST-DEALER RELATIONSHIP

Numerous states (at least twenty thus far including California and New York) have passed laws governing the consignment relationship between artist and dealer. These laws are generally similar in that they establish a trust relationship (involving the highest degree of responsibility and fairness) between consignor (the artist) and consignee (the dealer) whenever an artist delivers one of his own original works to a dealer for the purpose of exhibition or sale. These statutes deem both the art and the proceeds from the sale of the art to be "trust property" held by the dealer for the artist. The effect of these laws is to protect the artist against the dealer's creditors who might otherwise have access to the dealer's inventory and proceeds in the case of the dealer's insolvency or failure to pay debts. Without these laws, such inventory and proceeds would ordinarily include the artwork received from artists on consignment.

If you have work on consignment with dealers in states where such laws have not yet been passed (check with an arts organization in the state where the dealer is located; see Chapter 9) your only recourse in the event of your dealer's insolvency may be self-help. In such a situation self-help is little more than removing your artwork from the dealer's premises before he goes belly up. But a word of caution! If you have good reason to believe your dealer is in financial trouble, you should consult an attorney before taking any self-help action. If you make a mistake and your dealer is in fact able to continue in business, you may be facing a lawsuit for breach of contract. An attorney should be able to advise you on the extent of risk, if any, in using self-help.

The amount of protection any of the consignment laws provide to an artist will vary from state to state. For example, the California law (Civil Code sections 1738 to 1738.9) requires the consignee (dealer) to be responsible for the loss of, or damage to, the work of art after delivery of the work. The New York law (Article 12 of the N.Y. Arts and Cultural Affairs Law) is silent on this issue. The California law, however, appears to exclude photographic prints from the protection of the law while the New York statute expressly includes prints made from photographic negatives.

Finally, you should be aware that some states such as New York and California have strict laws governing disclosures to buyers of multiples. Consignors and dealers must specify such information about a multiple as the size of the edition, whether it is a restrike, the medium, etc. Dealers are required to post signs in their galleries advising the public that they may demand such data about a prospective purchase. Even if your contract with your dealer does not require you to provide such information, you should do so in writing for each multiple you sell and you should require your dealer to pass the accurate information along to all shoppers.

We urge you to make an effort to find out if there is an art consignment law in the state where your current or prospective dealer is located. If you know what your rights are before you enter into a relationship with an art dealer, you will be in a better position to protect yourself during the relationship. If you are already represented by a dealer, you will still be better off knowing what your rights are in the event the relationship proves unsatisfactory.

4

REPRODUCTIONS AND PUBLICATIONS

Reproductions of a visual artist's works are needed for a wide range of purposes: retail sales, publicity to sell originals, scholarship, charity, gallery inventory, portfolios, and so on. An artist should manage his rights to reproduce each of his own works differently, depending on the purpose of the reproduction. The information in Chapter 1 about copyright should be reviewed carefully in connection with negotiations over reproduction rights. Except for the extent to which an artist conveys reproduction rights to others, or unless the copyright has been lost or expired, an artist owns the exclusive rights to reproduce his original works. This chapter examines the practical aspects of conveying and managing those rights.

PHOTOGRAPHS

A photograph of a work of art results in the creation of a negative and a positive image of that negative. The law treats both equally. If the photograph is simply a record image of the primary work of art, without embellishment or interpretation, the reproduction rights in the photograph belong to the person who owns them in the primary work of art. The physical object of the photograph (both the negative and positive), lacks adequate originality to be copyrightable. If the artist still owns the reproduction rights in the primary artwork, he should be able to control the distribution and use of the photographs of his work. The photographer should be compensated for his service just as a framer would be for framing a painting.

The photographer in such circumstances may hold a different view of the matter and may treat the photograph as a work of art itself. If he embellishes the photograph (by adding a decorative border, for example), or in some other way contributes enough originality to it that it is worthy of copyright, indeed he may have a separate work of art over which he alone controls reproduction. If he has the artist's consent to reproduce the principal work of art in his secondary work (the photograph), the artist may not sue the photographer for violating the artist's reproduction rights. How much originality is enough is a difficult question with no clear answer. Therefore, the artist and photographer should agree in writing in advance about this matter.

Written agreements with photographers are extremely important because many photographers will not release the negatives of photographs; thus they often retain physical, if not legal, control over reproduction of the primary work of art. Some state statutes specify that the materials of production, e.g., photographic negatives, belong to the contractor who performs the work unless the parties agree to another arrangement. Such statutes, however, do not affect the ownership of reproduction rights, which is controlled exclusively by federal law.

QUALITY CONTROL

Just as with the right to reproduce artwork, the quality standards for reproductions should also be reduced to writing between the parties involved. They probably cannot agree in advance on what is good enough, but they probably can agree in advance on who should make the decision and how. An artist may be more widely known by reproductions of his work than by the originals. Poor quality reproductions can create a poor image of an artist's work. In a contract with a publisher who will be distributing books, slides, gifts, postcards, posters, or other reproductions of an artist's work, the artist should retain the right to approve personally and sign or initial approval of the proofs. For color reproductions, this is extremely important because of the possibility of inaccurate color or registration in the printing process. A sculptor will have other concerns about the best angle from which to photograph the object, the best background and shadows, and the accuracy of a three dimensional reproduction.

An artist may inadvertently waive his right to control the quality of reproductions by failing to emphasize this right in a contract. A gallery contract may authorize the gallery to make and distribute reproductions for publicity purposes. A publication contract may give the author or publisher responsibility to identify and photograph the works to be published. These clauses of such agreements should include clear language establishing which party will exercise quality control, time deadlines for approvals, maximum numbers of proofs the publisher is willing to furnish and any special involvement the artist is to have in the manufacturing process.

CONTEXT

An artist may be pleased to have his works reproduced on posters but not on cocktail napkins or handbags. Although after the fact an artist may be able to sue a manufacturer who publishes the artwork in a circumstance which the artist considers degrading, an artist may prevent such a problem by being specific in the written agreement conveying reproduction rights. The current law in the United States will not be sympathetic to an artist whose paintings suddenly appear in a pornography magazine if the artist conveyed to the publisher unlimited rights to reproduce his artwork.

Publication

If Guido the painter conveys reproduction rights to a book publisher by means of an agreement that gives the publisher all rights to reproduce Guido's two masterpieces, the publisher then owns those rights and he may sell them or assign part of them to a third party. To prevent this situation, Guido must be certain that he conveys only a license to the publisher. The licensing contract should tightly limit the purposes for which he is conveying reproduction rights to the publisher. Guido should insist that the contract state which objects may be reproduced, in what form, for how long, in how many editions of how many issues each, whether the publisher may reconvey those rights, the nature of the publications in which the reproductions will appear and other similar restrictions. Loose language may result in unpleasant surprises. If Guido's contract states that the publisher may publish reproductions of "all of Guido's pastel drawings," Guido may paint more than two pastel drawings and the publisher may demand to reproduce them even though at the time of the contract Guido only had two pastel drawings in his studio. Contracts should be specific about objects to which they refer.

Owners of the Object

United States law does not require that an artist convey reproduction rights along with the object itself. If an object is under copyright and the artist sells it, the new owner acquires the artwork only, not the right to reproduce it. A careful buyer will demand that the artist assign him copyright, however. If the artist does convey copyright to the new owner, he can do so partially or entirely. The conveyance çan be conditioned on whatever terms the parties can negotiate. (See Chapter 1 on Copyright.) Among the rights conveyed may be the right to make reproductions.

If a candy manufacturer buys from Guido his painting of a box of candy and makes clear to Guido that the painting will be hung in the company board room and reproduced as the company logo, Guido may find that the painting itself is worth only a fraction of the value of its reproduction rights. If the manufacturer buys the painting and obtains an unconditional assignment of copyright from Guido, the manufacturer is free to use the painting in any way he chooses except insofar as Guido may have moral rights or preservation rights (see Chapter 7). Therefore, Guido should learn as much as possible about the future uses of his artwork and not undervalue the reproduction rights.

It is important for all artists to keep in mind the distinctions among the various exclusive rights that comprise the copyright in a work of art. You may find that a customer or patron who asks you to transfer the copyright in the work does not necessarily want or need all the exclusive rights. Where the reproduction, distribution and display rights are the main concern of the customer, you may be able to grant a license rather than convey complete ownership in those rights. Furthermore, you may be able to avoid conveying any interest in your right to create a derivative work if that client does not have a genuine need to exercise that right.

A successful artist who already knows the value of reproductions of his work will probably have developed a standard copyright assignment form which he will offer to patrons who insist on having some amount of copyright ownership. Such a form will probably limit the purposes for which reproductions can be made or used. The more the artist limits the patron, however, the lower the price for the object may be.

Once an artist sells his work to a patron, he loses control over who owns it next and on what terms; if the artist still holds reproduction rights, he may be able to control reproduction. The patron who buys the object from the artist may sell, loan or give it to anyone he chooses unless he has agreed with the artist in advance to limit his future conveyances. This reflects our basic American respect for the rights of property owners. Statutes are being enacted to preserve some rights for artists as their works change hands, such as the royalty right discussed in Chapter 7. It is still basically true that an artist's protection must be by agreement at the time of the first sale. Because there is no legal "relationship" between the artist and future owners (as there is between artist and client) the artist cannot contractually limit the uses those future owners make of the object.

5

LEASES

Most artists rent real property in which to live or work or both. This chapter concerns the basic legalities of being a tenant or lessee. (We refer to "real property" which is the land and permanent improvements on it; the "lessor" is the "landlord"; the "lessee" is the tenant.) Being both an artist and a tenant may cause some special legal problems. For the most part, however, an artist who has signed a lease simply has the legal problems of any lessee of real property. The most common problems in this area of the law afflict artists who consider their homes to be their studios also. The law frequently takes a different view of the situation.

In the United States, property owners can convey to other parties all or something less than the entire interest in the property which they own. A lease of real property is usually such a conveyance: The owner leases to the tenant the right to use certain property on certain terms for a certain period of time. A lease is both a contract and a special right to use real property. It is therefore governed by both contract law and property law. Leases for the use of real property should always be in writing.

No one can lease to anyone else any greater right to use the property than he himself has. For example, if Guido the painter owns an easement across a parcel of property for the specific purpose of constructing, using and maintaining his driveway, he can lease to Skeezix the sculptor that easement but no greater property right in that strip of land. He cannot lease to Skeezix the right to build an airplane runway across that same strip of land if the easement's specific purpose is limited to a driveway for road vehicles. Similarly, if Guido owns Building No. 1, but not Building No. 2 next door, he can lease to Skeezix nothing more than Building No. 1 and no part of Building No. 2. This seems obvious, but the point is that as a tenant an artist should be extremely careful to lease property from someone who owns all of the rights and interests which are being conveyed to the artist. This works the other way around, too. In situations in which property can be sublet by the tenant, i.e., leased out by the tenant to a third party, the original tenant may sublease only the property interest he possesses. If an artist leases a loft from the landlord for one year, the artist can sublease to his brother for a period of time no greater than remains on the original one-year lease.

NEGOTIABILITY

A second and very important guiding principle of leases is the fact that they are negotiable. In this respect, they show their contractual features. There is no such thing as a standard lease just as there is no such thing as a standard contract. Most stationery stores sell basic form leases. A prospective tenant should buy such an example of a lease, read it and understand it. It is not necessary to sign a lease which looks like that one, however. Nor is it necessary to sign exactly the lease which a landlord proposes to any tenant, or vice verse. As with contracts, this is a matter to be determined by bargaining power.

Problems arise not when the parties have agreed carefully in writing to all of the terms of the lease but instead when the parties have been too casual about the arrangement. Failure to reduce a lease in writing to include all of what each of the parties understands individually to be the terms of the lease is foolish. If a conflict arises, the law takes over and generally dictates what the terms of the lease are to the extent the landlord and tenant fail to write their agreement. Under these circumstances, neither party may be satisfied with the outcome. Thus, it is all the more important to commemorate a lease to writing if special terms come into play.

IMPROVEMENTS

Unless the parties agree to the contrary, a tenant who makes permanent improvements to the structure which he leases may be required to leave those fixtures and improvements behind when he departs the building or else buy them back from the landlord and leave the building in repaired condition. In some states, however, the law distinguishes between trade fixtures and residential fixtures. Be sure to check whether your state law allows a departing tenant to take either type of fixture with him, and be sure that your lease specifies which type of fixture is at issue.

For example, if an artist rents raw space and refinishes the interior of the space during the term of the lease (puts up walls, paints, replaces flooring, installs a bathroom and a darkroom, etc.), such installations probably belong to the landlord. Thus, the artist may not remove them upon the expiration of the lease or demand to be paid for them. This is an area of common misunderstandings between artists and landlords but one which displays the power of property ownership in the United States. It is not unusual for an artist to be able to afford to rent only the least expensive space but nevertheless to feel taken advantage of by a landlord who benefits from the artist's hard work at fixing the property. Before entering into such an agreement, an artist should understand that unless the parties agree that the artist will somehow be compensated for his efforts (such as by extremely low rent), those fixtures and improvements can be a windfall for the landlord.

RENT CONTROL

Another major area of concern for artists is rent control. Rent control is a creature of legislation. There is no basic right to a controlled rent, except insofar as the city, county or state in which the property is located has enacted a law specifically prohibiting the landlord from raising the rent beyond a certain amount. Rent control statutes and ordinances are common in large metropolitan areas in the United States, but any prospective tenant should check very carefully to determine whether in fact the rent on his property is controlled and what the terms of such control are. Currently, some local rent control ordinances are being attacked in the courts and some legislatures are overturning them—the California Legislature, for example, passed a recent statute making most commercial rent control ordinances illegal.

Rent control statutes and ordinances vary widely. Some of them control only property in residential zones; others govern commercial rents. Some permit the landlord to raise the rent to fair market value when one tenant moves out and the next tenant moves in. Some rent control ordinances, however, control the amount for which the landlord can rent the property even upon re-rental to a new tenant. The economics of rental property are such that landlords typically will not make expensive investments in improving property which is subject to extreme forms of rent control. It is impossible for them to fully amortize their investment in a short enough period of time. These communities may be fertile fields for a starving artist looking for low rent.

ZONING AND PERMITS

It is common for artists to move into marginal or depressed neighborhoods to take advantage of low rents. After a few years of cleanup and fixup by artist tenants, owners of such property frequently experience an increase in fair market value of their property. Escalating rents force artists out, ironically denying them the property which they themselves helped to make valuable. The modern answer to this problem is specialized zoning for artists. In large cities especially, ordinances have been used to protect the rights of artists to inhabit large, open loft areas made out of former manufacturing spaces. An artist looking for housing should consult the local zoning and planning authorities to find such areas where his investments will be protected.

While zoning may offer such opportunities to artists, as noted above, zoning or other land-use restrictions can present them with problems as well. Any artist negotiating a lease with a landlord should inquire about all restrictions on the use of the property and determine whether such restrictions are consistent with the artist's needs. For a painter or artist who works in pastels or pencil, this is less likely to be a problem than for an artist using machinery or hazardous materials. An artist creating large sculptures and other works of extreme weight or that are likely to physically stress the leased property should consult the proposed lease carefully and talk with the local planning and zoning office before agreeing to rent the property. A landlord may be well within his rights in evicting a tenant who has rented the property for a residence and/or studio but who is in fact using the space as something more akin to a factory.

Any successful artist who is working out of his studio is effectively running a business in that space, especially if he sells his works there. In addition to observing the municipal zoning and planning ordinances, it may be necessary for the artist to obtain a business license. Some cities have ordinances prohibiting the use of residential property for any form of business. Any artist who may find himself hammering late into the night or playing loud music or otherwise attracting attention to himself should think long and hard about moving into a neighborhood where his "business" may not be welcome or legal.

Some uses of property are permitted "as of right." This means no special permission is necessary to conduct certain activities in certain locations. Other uses may require a permit or a variance. For example, a city ordinance may state that buildings on Main Street are historic and therefore no one may alter the facade of a building on Main Street without a permit. An artist who rents a building on Main Street and decides to put in a new window to improve the light in his studio could face a citation or even a lawsuit for replacing the window without obtaining the required permit. A conditional use permit might be necessary to use a garage as an artist's studio in a particular neighborhood. Violating ordinances of this type could cause the artist's studio to be declared a nuisance. A lawsuit could be brought to force the artist to abandon his studio or discontinue his use of the space for that purpose. Nevertheless, unless the artist has a carefully negotiated lease in which the landlord plainly leased the garage to the artist for the sole purpose of use as a workshop, or—better still—in which the landlord warranted to the artist that the artist's intended use was legal and required no permits, the artist could be required to continue paying rent to the landlord even though the law would not allow the artist to use it as his workshop.

Some uses are simply forbidden. Sometimes the owner or landlord forbids certain conduct on the property; sometimes local ordinances flatly prohibit certain uses of land; at other times deed restrictions which only the neighbors can enforce prohibit certain uses of property. For an example of the latter, residential suburban neighborhood property may be subject to a deed restriction prohibiting anyone in the area from parking a recreational vehicle in front of his house. In some planned developments, the deed restrictions can be very comprehensive. In all cases where an artist plans to rent property, he should determine in advance whether he is legally permitted to use it as he plans.

RENT PAYMENTS

Rent money and the frequency of payment seem to be simple aspects of leasing property but an artist should think carefully and creatively about these matters. Most states have laws governing landlord and tenant relationships, particularly as they relate to the term of a lease and the rent, but the law does not require a tenant to pay any specific amount of rent or to adhere to any specific cycle. Once the parties establish a pattern, the law will generally regard it as agreed upon. If the parties have no written lease accurately describing their legal rights, a court resolving a dispute will consider the evidence presented and determine those rights based on what the parties appear to be doing.

Rent is usually paid in the form of money, i.e., a check to the landlord. Alternate forms of rental payments are perfectly legal. An artist and landlord can agree that the artist will install a new kitchen in exchange for one year of rent-free possession of the property, or that the artist will give the landlord a particular painting in exchange for rent-free possession. Unusual agreements of this type are particularly prone to dispute and should therefore always be in writing. The written lease should state what kind of kitchen or exactly which painting. The lease should be as specific as possible about the details of the transaction.

A tenancy can be for a specific period of time (such as one year) at a lump sum rental amount, to be paid periodically, such as monthly or quarterly. The tenancy itself can be periodic, perhaps month-to-month as evidenced by the tenant's payment in advance to the landlord of the predetermined amount of money due to cover that period. When either party to a periodic tenancy wants to change the rent or terminate the arrangement, notice to the other party must be given one period in advance unless the parties agree to some other plan in writing. So, for a month-to-month tenancy, the tenant pays the landlord at the beginning of each month for that month. The landlord must advise the tenant at least one month in advance that he is cancelling the lease. If the period is two months, the tenant pays the rent at the start of each two-month period and two months' notice is required to terminate.

The significant difference between a periodic tenancy with rent due at short intervals and a fixed tenancy with one amount due, but payable in small units, is that terminating the latter early can be far more expensive for the tenant. The landlord can require the tenant to pay all the remaining rent, especially if the landlord cannot find a substitute tenant, even if the tenant terminating the agreement makes no further use of the property. Terminating a periodic tenancy subjects the tenant to liability for the rent for the last period only.

DAMAGE DEPOSITS

As mentioned above, most states have laws generally governing relations between landlords and tenants of residential property, especially to the extent that the parties do not agree in writing to the contrary. Damage deposits are commonly governed by such statutes, but read the law carefully to determine whether it applies to a lease for workshop space or only to residential rentals. Some state laws are heavily influenced by property owners or landlords. Other more consumer-oriented states have laws that are more protective of tenants. Thus, it is impossible to generalize about what the state law on this subject provides but an artist should check carefully for his statutory rights.

It is quite common for a tenant to give the landlord the first and last months' rents at the time of signing the lease. The last month's rent is a prepayment, the landlord's assurance against a tenant terminating the lease without prior notice. A security or damage deposit is not rent. Instead, a security deposit is money deposited by the tenant with the landlord to be used by the landlord, after the tenant moves out, to repair damage to the property. Often a landlord will request that a tenant provide a deposit equal to the rent for one month. The law alone does not require a tenant to make any damage deposit, nor is any set amount required. The landlord generally establishes this requirement, but it is negotiable.

If a written lease is involved, it should also operate as written receipt for all up-front money given to the landlord by the tenant. It should state clearly that the tenant gave the landlord a certain sum for the first month's rent, a separate sum for the last month's rent (if he did so), and yet another sum as a damage deposit if appropriate. In the unfortunate situation in which the parties do not execute a written lease, the tenant should write separate checks for these items, noting the purpose of the payment on each check.

Generally, a landlord is under no legal obligation to pay interest on the damage deposit, although the parties are free to agree on interest due to the tenant. In some states, a landlord is not even required to refund any of the deposit unless the tenant, having moved out, makes a prompt written demand. In other states, the landlord must send the tenant a letter promptly after the tenant vacates the premises, itemizing all damage for which the deposit is being used, or else refund it in full. In some states, the damage deposit may not be used to offset unpaid rent. Also, the type of damage which the landlord may assess against the deposit is often limited, so that ordinary wear and tear may not be included. A tenant is always liable for the full amount of actual damage he does to the property, regardless of the amount of the deposit, unless the landlord has agreed in writing that he will not hold the tenant responsible for damage in excess of a certain amount, a rare situation. Landlords can and do sue tenants who leave a mess behind. New landlords often contact former landlords for a tenant's references, thus making it a good idea to leave property in condition at least as good as that in which the property was found at the start of the tenancy.

One man's meat is another man's poison. If a tenant paints a mural on the bedroom wall which the landlord finds offensive, the landlord may be well within his property law rights in hiring a house painter to cover the mural with white paint and charging that cost to the tenant when the tenant moves out. In states which have enacted art-preservation statutes, discussed below in Chapter 7, a legal conflict may exist over the artist's continuing rights in his mural and the landlord's property rights. A better example might be a case in which an artist tenant paints the wooden living room floor purple and the landlord assesses against the artist's deposit the cost of refinishing the living room floor. Because accidents may occur in an artist's workspace, it is especially important to reach agreement with the landlord in advance over the condition in which the landlord expects his property to be left when the tenant departs.

SUBLEASES AND ROOMMATES

Landlords may but are not required to allow tenants to sublease property to parties other than the tenants themselves. Some leases indicate that subleasing is prohibited; others state that the landlord must first consent in writing. In the latter situation, obtaining the landlord's consent may amount to negotiating a new lease. The critical reason a landlord may want the primary tenant to remain a tenant under the lease, even though the tenant subleases to a subtenant, is that if the subtenant defaults on the obligation to pay rent, damages the property or otherwise violates the provisions of the lease, the landlord can hold the primary tenant fully responsible. Translated for the tenant, this means one should carefully avoid subleasing property unless that property is truly unique and worth keeping for possible future use even at a potentially high cost.

If the primary tenant subleases the property at a profit to himself, that is if he collects more rent than he pays the landlord, it may be worthwhile to sublease space. Such windfalls are rare these days because most landlords demand all the benefit of the higher rent. If an artist rents raw space, fully improves it, then subleases it, however, the landlord need not allow the artist to enjoy the fruits of his labors by collecting more rent than he pays. In a renter's market, on the other hand, where rental rates are declining and vacancy rates are high, a tenant may have to sublease his space at a loss because the landlord holds him fully responsible for the agreed rental but the sublessee will not pay as much rent.

Roommates are not necessarily subtenants. If Guido and Skeezix want to share a studio they decide to rent from Lucy, both Guido and Skeezix should sign the lease as co-tenants. This leaves each of them equal rights in the lease, but they share full liability. For example, if Guido leaves town one day, Skeezix still owes Lucy all the rent. After Guido moves out and sends word that he will never be back, Skeezix may decide he needs to split the rent with someone else, so he may invite Robert to be his "roommate." Robert is not a co-tenant because he did not sign the original lease with Lucy. Instead, Robert is a subtenant.

Such arrangements are common but should be formalized in writing to preserve the expectations of the parties. The original lease between Guido, Skeezix and Lucy may state plainly that only Guido and Skeezix are permitted to share the studio. Lucy may not want Robert in the building. In a situation where no one else is liable or welcome to share the property with Skeezix, he and/or Lucy may wish or be compelled to sue Guido for breaching the lease. Many buildings are regulated as to how many people may occupy them, whether children or pets are allowed, and so on. A sublessor or co-tenant may find himself responsible for the acts of his sublessee or co-tenant.

6

FINANCIAL CONSIDERATIONS— BUSINESS FORM, TAXES, AND WILLS

This chapter examines the major legal concerns facing an artist who has begun to experience, or is already accustomed to, financial success— money issues. Although many people prefer to ignore these problems, they deserve attention at the earliest possible date to avoid legal trouble down the road. Any artist suddenly selling his work at high prices should immediately consult a certified public accountant and possibly a tax attorney to assure that the artist's financial books are well organized and to prevent future problems.

BUSINESS FORM

SOLE PROPRIETORSHIP

An artist who makes and sells artwork is in business and, as discussed in Chapter 5, may need a business license from his city. A basic business operation such as this is known as a sole proprietorship. In a sole proprietorship, funds can flow directly into and out of the owner's treasury with no significant distinction between the business and the owner. The income of the business is the income of the owner. This is the simplest form of doing business.

The name of the artist will automatically be the name of the business because he *is* the business, unless he decides to do business under a fictitious name. For example, a painter may sign and sell his works under a pseudonym such as "Guido" even though the artist himself is named John Jones. In such a case, the artist should file a fictitious name statement with the local government and usually publish a legal notice in the newspaper explaining to the public that John Jones is doing business as Guido at a certain address. In this way, Guido may have a checking account, order supplies, etc. in that name.

For most artists, a sole proprietorship is a satisfactory business form. There are alternatives, however, which a sophisticated transaction may require. The two major alternatives are corporation and partnership. An artist may incorporate himself, i.e., form a corporation which he owns and directs, or he may enter into a partnership with other people or business entities.

CORPORATION

In the eyes of the law, a corporation is a legal person with rights of its own. It may do whatever its organizers authorize it to do. Generally, a corporation may buy and sell property, sue and be sued, make and receive loans, issue stock, and so on. A corporation must pay its own taxes, also, except for a special type of corporation known as an "S corporation" which pays its federal taxes through its owner. The principal advantage of a corporation is that it offers a shield from liability for the owners. For example, if John Jones incorporates himself as Guido Inc. and Guido Inc. is sued by Central Art Supplies, Guido Inc. may have to pay the plaintiff Central Art Supplies but John Jones' personal assets usually will be inaccessible to the plaintiff. Central Art Supplies was doing business with Guido Inc., not with John Jones personally. The corporate form has other advantages, such as the fact that a corporation can deduct from its federal income tax the state income tax it pays whereas an individual may not do so.

The corporate wall between the owners and the corporation is not impenetrable, however. The law has developed many exceptions to the protection a corporation offers its owners. These exceptions are particularly important for artists contemplating incorporation because an incorporated artist would likely be the sole owner, director and officer of his corporation and could easily forget to observe the wall between himself and the corporation. In general, the courts will not pierce the corporate wall if the corporation is well capitalized, i.e. has enough equity, has regular meetings, pays regular salaries to the officers and other employees, pays dividends to shareholders and observes the other corporate formalities such as holding regular meetings, keeping minutes, and so on. The major disadvantage to most sole incorporators of this form of business is that the corporation pays income tax on its income and all shareholders must pay income tax again on dividends, as must all officers and other employees on their salaries. This double taxation, together with the bookkeeping and paperwork problems of the corporate form, make it worthwhile for rather few artists. A corporation may well be advisable, however, for financially successful artists who might otherwise have substantial personal assets exposed in the event of a lawsuit or for artists commissioned to fabricate and install large works of art in public places where there is greater likelihood of a personal injury lawsuit.

PARTNERSHIP

A partnership, on the other hand, is a group of two or more parties (either people or business entities such as corporations) formed to share the benefits and liabilities of the venture. If two artists, Guido and Skeezix, decide to collaborate on a large mobile commissioned for an airport, a partnership may be well advised. Under the terms of a written partnership agreement, the partners agree who will do what work and what percentage of income and liability goes to each. Income and liabilities flow directly through the partnership to the partners themselves according to the terms of the partnership. Taxes are paid only once, by the partners, not the partnership. The principal disadvantage of a partnership is that each of the partners is liable to third parties for all the liabilities of the partnership. For example, if Guido dies while the work is under construction, Skeezix alone is responsible for all the costs of supplies not yet paid for. Under the terms of the partnership agreement, of course, Guido may have been required to obtain a life insurance policy payable to Skeezix for precisely such a situation. The supplier looking to be paid, however, needs to look only as far as Skeezix if the supplies were sold to the partnership. There is one type of partnership known as a limited partnership in which some of the partners can limit their liability and others may be what are called general partners. The general partners are those responsible for the day-to-day management of the project, however, and thus would probably include an artist in an art project.

Before selecting and forming his business entity, an artist should itemize on paper all of his expectations and needs from his business, then seek an attorney's help in drafting the appropriate documents. Particularly in organizing a corporation or partnership, the drafting of documents can be a complex task which an attorney can do efficiently. Do-it-yourself books and kits are available, however, for this purpose. If you choose the latter approach, be sure to spend enough time with the materials to distinguish your situation from those in the models or examples. Be thorough and you won't be sorry.

TAXES

A professional artist generating income by selling his work must be concerned with federal and state income taxes as well as sales tax. It is important to note, however, that tax law changes very rapidly and varies from jurisdiction to jurisdiction. Sales tax, for example, is a matter of state and local law. Consulting a certified public accountant as soon as financial success seems probable is extremely important for artists. Tax planning requires thinking in advance to avoid ugly surprises at the time tax returns are due, or at the time of an audit.

Every artist should know that he can obtain free advice, without revealing his name, by simply phoning the Internal Revenue Service. The IRS offers toll-free telephone assistance in every state and will mail, at no charge, any of its numerous publications explaining the tax law, which is updated regularly. One can also walk into the nearest IRS office and obtain a free consultation. Post offices and public libraries usually have blank tax return forms available for filing with the IRS and the state tax authority.

A United States citizen or resident must file a federal income tax return reporting his taxable income with the IRS, even if that person actually owes no tax, provided certain minimum standards apply to that person: A single person (as of the last day of his tax year, December 31 for most people) under 65 years of age must file a return if his gross earned income was at least a certain amount during the year ($4,950 for 1988). A self-employed person of any age, however, which includes most professional artists, must file a tax return (1040 SE) along with Schedule C if his net earnings from the business are $400 or more during the year. Thus, if Skeezix sells one sculpture for which his net earnings are $400 or more for the year, he must file a federal tax return regardless of other income. Self-employment in a trade or business, even as a part-time occupation—as in the case of an artist who works in a restaurant daily but paints at night and regularly sells his paintings—results in separate business income on which taxes must be paid. Schedule C is for this separate business income whether it is one's full- or part-time occupation. Anyone having more than one business must file a separate schedule C for each business. A self-employed person must also pay self-employment tax, which is the social security for self-employed individuals. For 1988, this is a 13.05% tax on the gross profits of the business as shown on Schedule C.

Not everyone files the same type of income tax return form with the IRS. The correct form to be submitted by a taxpayer depends on his personal circumstances, such as marital status or total income. Only one form should be submitted. The forms, from least to most complex, are 1040 EZ, 1040A, and 1040. Any artist wishing to deduct expenses like the cost of canvas and paint from his gross income must file form 1040. Schedules such as Schedule C are attached to these returns to show the income and expenses of self-employment. Depending on the amount of self-employment income and the percentage of it to total income, an artist may be required to file quarterly tax returns, depositing taxes on estimated income. An artist who has a business, i.e. is an owner rather than a paid employee of any business, must obtain from the IRS an employer-identification number, even if the only "employee" of the business is himself. Upon doing so, the artist will receive coupons for estimated tax deposits. In addition to tax returns, businesses must file certain information returns with the IRS for barter-exchange transactions, for payments of $600 or more to independent contractors, or for payments over $10,000 received in cash.

Determining reportable income and deductible expenses (adjusted gross income) is often a problem. An artist must total gross income and may deduct from it only certain expenses to arrive at the taxable amount. The income column must include all income received—wages, tips, salaries, interest, bonuses, dividends, proceeds of sales (e.g., on paintings), unemployment compensation, cancelled debt, most prizes, gambling winnings, and so on. Certain funds received are not currently taxable income, however, and therefore need not be reported, for example life insurance proceeds, military allowances, interest on state or local bonds, gifts or inheritances, child support payments, social security benefits, worker compensation payments, welfare benefits, and veterans' benefits.

The taxpayer may subtract from this income figure limited amounts of money spent on certain activities, including moving expenses, employee business expenses, retirement plan contributions, alimony paid, expenses for maintaining rental property owned for a business purpose, depreciation of rental property owned for a business purpose, certain travel expenses (including car expenses if a car is needed for work), certain medical and dental expenses, certain interest payments, charitable contributions, significant nonbusiness casualty and theft losses, certain educational expenses, dues to professional societies, small tools and supplies used for work, subscriptions to professional journals and trade magazines, work clothes and uniforms, legal and accounting fees, investment fees and expenses, and more. Currently, the IRS takes the position that artists may deduct 50% of production expenses in the year they are incurred and then deduct 25% in each of the following two years, or amortize the expenses over the period in which income is received. Congress may make changes in the near future making this more favorable to artists.

Complex rules apply to each of these deductions, most notably the new 2% limit on several of them. The 2% limit permits a taxpayer to deduct only so much of his total "miscellaneous deductions" as equals more than 2% of his adjusted gross income. ("Miscellaneous deductions" are permitted for a limited category of expenditures, including investment expenses, union dues, professional books and publications, and nonreimbursable employee business expenses.) For example, painter Guido has adjusted gross income of $100,000 for the tax year, and after deductions his adjusted gross income is $84,000. He spent a total of $2,000 on miscellaneous deductibles such as tax advice. The 2% limit will entitle him to miscellaneous deductions totalling only $320—which is $2,000 minus $1,680 (2% of $84,000).

Just like other taxpayers, artists are permitted to deduct certain charitable contributions from total gross income provided the taxpayer itemizes his deductions (and therefore files form 1040). Charitable contributions may be money or property so long as the contribution is made to a charity with proper tax-exempt status. If the contribution is valuable property rather than cash (something other than the artist's own work), the taxpayer must accompany his tax return with IRS form 8283, which requires an appraisal of the property.

For artists and other taxpayers who create objects which they subsequently give away to qualified charities, the amount of the deduction is limited to what is called the taxpayer's "basis" in the property for federal income tax purposes. This means that an artist who donates his own work to a qualified tax-exempt organization can deduct only the out-of-pocket expenses he incurred to form the basis of that artwork, such as the cost of paint and canvas or clay and bronze. No deduction is permitted in such a case for appreciation in value or for the artist's labor.

As an example, Guido has painted two large and very similar paintings, each worth $50,000. He sells one to Mrs. Patron for $50,000 and he contributes the other to the local museum, which has tax-exempt status. Mrs. Patron immediately donates her painting to another tax-exempt museum. Guido spent $300 on materials for each of the two paintings and $500 to frame each of them. He had no other costs or expenses directly attributable to these two paintings. Guido can deduct only $800 for his charitable contribution but Mrs. Patron can deduct $50,000 because that is her basis in the property and its current value is the same. Guido might be able to deduct from his state income taxes, however, the full fair-market value of his donated painting—$50,000. This depends on his state's income tax law. Congress may well restore to artists their ability to deduct the fair market value of their own works which they donate to qualified charities. Consult your congressman for an update.

Sales tax is a matter of state and sometimes local law. In most states, anyone selling personal property on a retail basis (i.e. to a consumer rather than a reseller), must collect sales tax from the buyer. The seller is responsible for collecting and paying this tax to the state. An artist selling artwork directly to customers falls into this category. States monitor such sales by periodically auditing businesses which have registered for licenses or by auditing the books of customers of artists. The obligation to collect and pay sales tax is often overlooked by artists, who are then subject to paying back taxes, interest and penalties. Only sales to resellers are exempt, unless of course the artist makes his sales in a state which levies no sales tax. Another common exemption is for sales to museums or other nonprofit organizations.

Artists are obliged to pay sales tax as well as collect it. In most states artists, as retail customers and consumers, must pay sales tax on the supplies and materials they purchase for fabricating their works.

WILLS

Any artist hopes that by the time of his death he will be so successful that he leaves behind a studio full of valuable artworks, royalties and other assets for his heirs. Preparing for this eventuality is essential and must be done regularly to update plans depending upon the condition of the artist's estate. Every professional artist will die leaving behind both finished and unfinished artworks, contractual rights and obligations, copyright and royalty rights together with other personal and real property and possibly debts. For artists who have achieved success by the time of their deaths, the value of their estates may escalate rapidly in the years immediately after death. What should be frightening about this process of preparing for death is the fact that anyone in the United States who dies without having left a valid will is what is known as "intestate," which means that the disposition of his property is governed by statute and not according to his wishes.

Probate law is strictly a matter of state law and generalizations can be extremely misleading. Note, however, that federal estate and gift tax law have a major effect on estate planning. Small estates generally do not incur tax liability. A federal estate tax return need be filed only for an estate with a gross value of $600,000 or more. (A spouse who inherits the whole estate need pay no tax but must file the return.) One huge success, however, can cause an obscure artist's estate suddenly to become large and create tax problems for his heirs.

There are two ways to make a will. The first and simplest (but riskiest) way is to write what is known as a holograph. A holographic will can be as simple as a handwritten statement on plain paper that "I, John Jones, hereby leave all of my property, real and personal, to my sister Annabel Smith. Dated July 1, 1988. Signed, John Jones." A holographic will must be entirely in the handwriting of the person making the will or the whole will may be held invalid. For example, if John Jones decides a month after writing the will quoted above that he would like to leave his two unfinished paintings of Central Park to his brother Robert, and puts his handwritten holographic will in the typewriter adding the gift to Robert in typing beneath his signature, the entire will would probably be invalid and he would be deemed to be intestate on death.

Handwriting one's will is risky business. Disgruntled heirs may attack a holograph as a fake or as written while the testator was under some strong influence, for example that he was drunk or sedated by medication. Because holographic wills have no witnesses, they are often challenged. In addition, any complicated disposition of property is one which generally does require the expertise of a lawyer familiar with the law governing wills and trusts in that particular state. Because of the possibility of destroying or invalidating a holograph or of improper drafting in the first place, few lawyers recommend holographic wills. We mention them because they are easy to make.

Alternatively a will can be typed or printed, signed by the testator (the person making the will) and witnessed by other people. Witnessed wills can be simple and inexpensive to have a lawyer prepare. Do-it-yourself will books may be helpful, also, as may be forms purchased from a stationery store. Whatever type of will is executed should be placed in an accessible location, not in a locked bank safety-deposit box. Copies can be made and distributed freely. A new will can and should state that it revokes all previous wills. A court must have the original, however, to open probate proceedings unless the court has proof that the original is lost.

People often ask whether they may omit someone from their wills. The answer is yes provided it is done carefully and expressly. Another common question is whether property *must* be left to certain relatives, for example to one's spouse. The answer is no. A will may accommodate the individual desires of the testator.

The law of wills and trusts includes many devices for providing for the survivors of the testator. An individual with young children or an elderly ailing parent can provide income for their care through the creation of a trust, either before or after death, either through a will or a separate trust instrument. A trust established during one's lifetime is a living trust, whereas a trust established under the terms of a will is a testamentary trust.

All wills should name an executor of the estate. An executor is someone who, upon the death of the testator, oversees administration of the decedent's affairs and assures that the terms of the will are carried out. Often the executor is the lawyer who drafts the will, although this is not at all necessary. One's surviving family members or best friend may be the executor.

An artist who dies leaving a studio full of valuable but unsold artwork requires an extremely trustworthy executor, someone who will oversee the careful disposition of those works for the benefit of the estate. Ask your executor if he or she would be willing to serve; provide in your will for that person to be compensated for his efforts and to be able to serve without bond (if you trust him or her implicitly, as you should before selecting the person); tell your chosen executor where you have stored your will and give him a copy of it; give him or her ready access to your possessions. It is especially wise to give the executor a regularly updated inventory of valuable possessions, including artworks.

At the time of his death, a successful artist is likely to be represented by at least one art dealer or gallery, which will probably have possession of a number of his works. During his lifetime, the wise artist would contemplate whether he wishes that representation agreement to survive him and who is to manage the disposition of his works, his gallery or his executor. Whatever the artist's plans, he should specify them in his will and in his agreement with the gallery. The famous case involving the estate of painter Mark Rothko illustrates that a consignee dealer of the deceased artist may face serious legal difficulties if he is also the executor of the artist's estate. Mark Rothko, a famous painter, died in 1970. His estate included nearly 800 of his paintings, of great value. The executors sold and consigned all the paintings quickly, but were subsequently held liable in money damages to Rothko's heirs because the executors were also connected with the art galleries to which the paintings were sold and consigned. The case, complicated and widely followed, spawned numerous magazine articles and at least one book.

The case above illustrates the major problem in appointing the artist's art dealer as executor of the artist's estate. An executor has fiduciary duties to the beneficiaries of the estate, and in the eyes of the law these are the most important. Serving two masters—the estate and his own gallery business—may create an impossible conflict of interest for a dealer/executor, which is best avoided by having different people perform these two functions.

7

MORAL RIGHT

Moral right, or "droit moral," comprises another bundle of rights associated with artists and authors. Droit moral evolved in Europe in the nineteenth and early twentieth centuries, but has only recently begun to be recognized in the United States. These rights are uniquely personal to the artist and, unlike copyright, cannot be transferred to another party.

Whereas copyright protects a property interest in a work of art that is distinct and separate from the physical object, moral right provides an artist with an ongoing relationship to the physical object itself. Artists are considered to have personality and reputational rights in their own artwork. Although there are numerous formulations of moral rights, the most frequently protected personal interests in countries recognizing the droit moral are the paternity right and the right of integrity.

The rights of both paternity and integrity have several dimensions. Generally speaking, the right of paternity entitles an artist to claim credit for his work under his own name or a pseudonym, if the artist so chooses. An artist's paternity right includes the corresponding rights to remain anonymous, to prevent misattribution of his work, and to disown a work which has been altered, damaged or displayed in a manner inconsistent with the artist's creative intent. The right of integrity enables an artist to protect the physical condition and presentation of his creative expression, regardless of who has actual possession or ownership of the work. The artist is thus able to prevent the mutilation, destruction, alteration or out-of-context display of his own work.

Although the extent of moral right protection may vary from one country to another, most European and many Latin American countries have recognized moral right to some degree. The paternity and integrity rights are even incorporated into the Berne Convention, which we covered earlier in our discussion of copyright. The United States, however, has been slow to recognize moral right for artists. In fact, the unwillingness of the United States to join the Berne Convention stems in part from resistance to the moral right requirement of the Convention.

This resistance is based largely on the historic strength of property rights in the United States and the mythical notion that the owner of personal property, such as a work of art, should be able to do with that object as he pleases. But the truth is that there are many limitations placed upon the use of property in the United States. Consider the impact of zoning, environmental and health and safety laws upon the use of personal property or real estate. In many communities homeowners may not freely change the exterior of their homes. An automobile may not lawfully be driven at sixty miles per hour on a residential street.

Fortunately, resistance to legal recognition of moral right is beginning to weaken. While artists in most states continue to do without moral rights protection, so far the states of Massachusetts, New York and California have taken limited but very positive steps toward creating a legal basis for recognizing and enforcing the moral rights of artists. With the possible exception of the termination right under the copyright law, the federal government has yet to take such action on behalf of artists. (As we write in early 1988, a bill to amend the Copyright law is pending in Congress. This bill, if enacted into law, would provide artists nationwide with both resale royalty rights and protection of the rights of paternity and integrity.)

Because so many artists in America (including Art Liveson, Skeezix D., and Guido Carpaccio) reside in New York or California, we will briefly review the moral rights protection afforded to artists in those states. Both the New York and California laws provide some measure of protection for both the rights of integrity and paternity, but there are important differences between them. The Massachusetts law essentially follows that of California, with one major exception which we will note below.

The California Art Preservation Act (Civil Code section 987) provides a right of integrity to artists by prohibiting anyone, with the exception of an artist in possession of his own work, from intentionally defacing, mutilating, altering or destroying a work of fine art. This prohibition extends to framers, conservators and restorers of art works who can be found liable if they act in such a way as to justify the belief that they were indifferent to the particular work of art. The Act even applies to works of art that are part of a building, unless the work cannot be removed from the building without substantial harm. An artist's right of paternity is also provided. An artist always "retains the right to claim authorship, or, for just and valid reason, to disclaim authorship of his or her work of fine art."

This is a very important law for California artists but it does have its limitations; some are major. The prohibitions of this Act apply only to "works of fine art," which this particular law defines as original paintings, sculptures, drawings or original works of art in glass. Works in other media (apparently including any work produced in limited edition multiples) are unprotected. As a result, many California artists are in a position similar to Skeezix D., a sculptor and photographer, who now has the right to protect the physical integrity of some of his artworks but not the others.

Protection under the California law is further limited to works "of recognized quality." A determination of recognized quality will be based upon the opinions of artists, art dealers, collectors of fine art, curators of art museums, and other persons involved in the creation or marketing of fine art. Whether this distinction will be unfairly applied in specific cases remains to be seen.

This law also exempts any work "prepared under contract for commercial use by its purchaser." The similarity of this provision to copyright ownership in a "work made for hire" is intentional. "Commercial use" is defined in the Art Preservation Act as fine art created under a "work made for hire" arrangement. Therefore, if the artist produces a work within the scope of his employment or enters into a written contract agreeing that the work is "made for hire," he will have no right of integrity in his work.

The right of paternity, unfortunately, also is affected by the limitations referred to above. Consequently, the area of least protection for paternity rights will be in the commercial context. An artist who produces an original work that would otherwise be covered by the paternity right will lose that right if his work is reproduced in any form. Furthermore, the paternity right would not apply to even a unique original work where the work was "prepared under contract for commercial use by its purchaser." So, for example, where Guido the painter produces an original painting on canvas in California, both the paternity right and right of integrity apply. If Guido licenses the painting to a company for reproduction and distribution, neither right would apply to the reproductions. Had Guido produced the canvas under a contract which provided for commercial use by the commissioning party, i.e., as a "work made for hire," even the unique original would be unprotected by either of the rights.

The California law also permits an artist to waive the rights of integrity and paternity under the Art Preservation Act if he does so in writing. As you can imagine, many artists with little bargaining power will be required to waive these rights as a condition of employment. It is likely that a written agreement to give up moral rights would also be binding on an artist in New York, even though the New York law is unclear on this point.

The New York Artists' Authorship Rights Act (Article 14-A of the N.Y. Arts and Cultural Affairs Law) differs in some significant ways from the California Act. The New York law protects the right of integrity by prohibiting anyone, except the artist or someone acting with the artist's consent, from either publicly displaying or publishing a work of fine art or its reproduction as the work of the artist when the work is altered, defaced, mutilated or modified and damage to the artist's reputation is reasonably likely to result. The California law by contrast does not limit its protection to public displays. In addition, the California law expressly prohibits destruction of works of fine art while the New York law does not. However, just as in California, the New York right of integrity also applies to art conservators; framers, however, are not included. The New York law also adopted the California exception for contract work produced for commercial purposes. In both states, the laws protecting works of art apply only to acts that take place in the individual state. New York has no authority over works of art in California and vice versa.

The range of art works protected in New York, however, is significantly broader than in California; the Massachusetts Moral Right Statute (Chap. 231, section 85S of the Mass. General Laws) is even broader than New York's. The New York law applies to "any original work of visual or graphic art of any medium" but excludes works of sequential imagery such as motion pictures. The right of paternity in the New York statute, which is essentially identical to that of California, does not extend to reproductions as the right of integrity does. The Massachusetts law covers "any original work of visual or graphic art of any media which shall include, but not [sic] limited to, any painting, print, drawing, sculpture, craft object, photograph, audio or video tape, film, hologram, or any combination thereof, of recognized quality."

With most legal rights, it is not always enough merely to be aware of their existence in order to benefit from them. On occasion, California and New York artists may have to demand that their rights of paternity and integrity be respected. As a last resort, an artist may contemplate bringing legal action, or, at least, threaten to do so. In the event a lawsuit is necessary to enforce the paternity or integrity rights, a prevailing artist in California (but not in New York) can recover, in addition to damages, attorney and expert witness fees. This is very favorable to artists because ordinarily a plaintiff is not entitled to recover these fees in a lawsuit.

In California, but not in New York, an artist's right of integrity and paternity survives for fifty years following that person's death and may be exercised by an artist's heirs or personal representative.

But what of artists in states that have not enacted moral rights laws? Do they have no protection whatsoever in this area? Not necessarily. There are generalized legal concepts such as defamation, invasion of privacy, and unfair competition which have been used to vindicate moral rights. Even the federal Lanham Act, which ordinarily applies to mislabeling of commercial packaged goods, has been used by artists to enforce a right of paternity. But these approaches to enforcing droit moral are difficult because they were not specifically developed to deal with artist's rights.

If you live in a state that has not adopted moral rights laws for artists, you can protect those rights to some degree by a written contract. In effect, you could condition the first retail sale of your work on the buyer's acceptance of some type of paternity and integrity rights. However, you probably could not bind subsequent purchases and sales of your work. As a practical economic matter, whether buyers of your work would be willing to enter into such an agreement will depend to some extent on your bargaining power. As we discussed in the contracts section, the sky's the limit as to what you can include in a written contract if demand for your work is great enough. But if you are a newcomer to the business side of the art world or you are not yet commercially successful, the chances are that you are not in a strong bargaining position. In that case, contracts might not provide you with much in the way of moral rights. In any event, you might consider lobbying your state legislature to enact legislation to protect artists' moral rights.

THE PUBLIC INTEREST IN PROTECTING WORKS OF ART

A unique feature of California law is the extension to public organizations of the artist's right of integrity. New York grants the right of integrity solely to the artist, and not to the artist's estate. Massachusetts allows the state Attorney General to assert the rights of a deceased artist, but only in regard to works of art in public view.

Section 989 of the California Civil Code extends the scope of the California Arts Preservation Act by enabling a non-profit arts-related organization to bring a lawsuit for injunctive relief (asking the court to order the defendant to perform an act or cease performing an ongoing or threatened act) to preserve or restore the integrity of a work of art with respect to intentional physical defacement, mutilation, alteration, or destruction. These rights also apply against framers, conservators and restorers for acts of gross negligence toward a work of art.

Under this statute, an arts-related non-profit organization may also bring a lawsuit to establish that a work of art may be removed from a building without substantial physical defacement, mutilation, alteration or destruction of the work, if the organization is prepared to pay for the removal. The organization may also exercise the same right as the artist or his heirs or personal representative in connection with art that is part of a building or structure. To encourage the exercise of these rights, the law permits the prevailing party in a lawsuit to recover attorneys' and expert witness fees. The court may also require the organization to post a bond.

The scope of fine art that is protected by this statute is narrower than the right of integrity directly exercised by an artist under section 987 of the Civil Code because section 989 applies only to works of "substantial public interest" while section 987 is not limited in that manner. Nevertheless, this statute theoretically provides a measure of additional protection for the reputation of some artists and also provides a vehicle to protect the public's interest in art.

One of the intriguing aspects of both sections 987 and 989 is that either the artist himself or an arts-related organization may bring legal action to protect works of art covered by these laws against a private collector as well as a public or private institution. This would include works of art that are not publicly displayed. For example, let's assume a collector owns a painted metal sculpture by a well known artist, which he privately displays on the grounds surrounding his residence. Assume further that he arranges to have the paint removed from the piece or simply has the piece painted a different color. There is a good chance that a lawsuit brought either by the artist or a qualified organization would result in a court order requiring the collector to incur the cost of restoring the piece to its original condition.

While the protection of a public interest in works of art may move us somewhat afield from the European concept of moral right, the ability of non-profit organizations to protect the physical integrity of works of art may ultimately prove as significant for the preservation of art as the efforts of other non-profit groups have been in protecting the environment.

ARTISTS' RESALE RIGHTS

Another form of artists' rights that exists widely in Europe is the right to profit from the resale of a work of art. This concept, which is frequently referred to as "droit de suite," varies considerably in application from country to country. The portion of proceeds to which the artist is entitled, whether the artist shares in gross proceeds or only in the net increase in value, and whether there is a minimum sales price that must be realized before the artist's right attaches to the sale, are issues that differ among nations.

The artists' resale right appears to be based conceptually upon two main assumptions: (1) an artist is more often than not exploited in the marketplace, and (2) the subsequent increase in value of a given work exists as a latent quality from the time of its creation as a result of the artist's skill. Whether or not one agrees with these statements, the concept of "droit de suite" has had a very cool reception in the United States.

Apart from the State of California, the artist's right to participate in the proceeds from the resale of his work is unrecognized in the U.S. This is true of both the laws of the individual states as well as the federal government, although a bill to extend this right to artists is before the United States Congress. American critics of the "droit de suite" are not limited to the dealers, collectors and auction houses, who stand to lose money if resale proceeds are shared with artists. Even artists, such as Guido Carpaccio and Skeezix D., are divided on whether such a right actually aids or hinders lesser known artists.

Guido is of the opinion that appreciation in value of an artist's work is the result of the artist's ongoing efforts, a byproduct of the recognition that the artist earns. To permit a dealer or collector to retain for himself the increase in value that results from resale would be to provide him with a windfall at the artist's expense.

Skeezix views the situation differently. He says that the percentage of artists in the United States who participate in a secondary market is minuscule. He believes that artists who are little known may be harmed by a resale right, because collectors may prefer to invest in the art equivalent of blue-chip stocks rather than gamble on a new artist where they will have the administrative hassle of locating the artist in order to pay him a portion of a small sale. Besides making a few well-off artists even better off, Skeezix thinks that a resale right may induce some artists to work for the market rather than follow their creative instincts.

In 1976, California took the bold step of passing into law the right of an artist to obtain a percentage of the proceeds from the resale of his work. The California legislature's action was unprecedented in the United States and, as we mentioned above, remains unique at both the state and federal level. The California law works this way: An artist is entitled to five per cent of the gross proceeds of the sale of one of his works of fine art if the seller resides in California or the sale takes place in California. Either the seller or the seller's agent is obligated to pay the artist. If the seller or his agent are unable to locate the artist within ninety days, the artist's proceeds are to be paid to the California Arts Council, which then has the obligation to locate the artist. Proceeds unclaimed after seven years are transferred to the Art in Public Buildings Program for use in making purchases of fine art.

If the seller fails to pay either the artist or the Arts Council, the artist may bring a lawsuit against the seller within three years of sale or one year from the date the artist discovers that the work has been sold. The prevailing party is entitled to payment of attorneys' fees by the loser.

There are some significant limits to the operation of this law. The resale right does not apply to initial sales of the work where the artist holds legal title at the time of the sale, or where the initial sale to the public is by a dealer who bought either from the artist or from another dealer. The right also does not apply where the gross proceeds from the sale are less than $1000 or where the resale price is less than the seller's purchase price. Moreover "fine art" is defined in this law as an original painting, sculpture, or drawing, or an original work of art in glass. Photography, prints and numerous other media are not covered. And where the sale is of a work of stained glass art permanently attached to a building, the right also does not apply. The law prohibits this right from being waived by the artist. In other words, even if the artist signs a contract agreeing not to require payment of the five per cent upon resale of the work, that part of the contract is invalid. The artist is still entitled to his percentage.

It is difficult to determine whether the California law has had much impact on artist-dealer relations. A 1986 survey conducted by Bay Area Lawyers for the Arts revealed that both California artists and dealers believe that resales covered by the law are few in number. The proposed amendment of the 1976 Copyright Act that we discussed earlier also includes a provision for artists' resale rights. Whether the California experience provides support for or against this bill remains to be seen.

This has been a very brief review of the concept of artists' moral rights in the United States and the means by which those rights may be enforced. If you need further information on whether and to what extent your rights of integrity and paternity are protected in your state, there are various possibilities for obtaining information free of charge. Most states and many cities have official or semi-official arts organizations, and many of these groups either produce publications on the subject or have knowledgeable individuals on their staffs to answer your questions. In addition, some cities and, in the case of California, one state have volunteer lawyers organizations dedicated to assisting artists. Under certain circumstances legal advice and even legal representation may be available to you at no cost. (See Chapter 9).

8

UNITED STATES CUSTOMS AND IMMIGRATION

CUSTOMS

Most artists who will read and use this book create and sell their works within the United States and would not ordinarily expect to deal with United States Customs. There are circumstances, however, where an American artist will come in contact with Customs laws and the question of the possible payment of duties. If an American artist, as a temporary resident in one or more foreign countries, produces works of art with which he returns to this country or which he ships back to the United States, the artist's work will pass through United States Customs. The same is true, of course, for a visiting artist from another country who either carries his work with him or exports his work to the United States. Many artists also collect works of art during their travels abroad with the intention of bringing these objects back to the United States. If any of these circumstances might apply to you, some basic knowledge about the Tariff Schedules of the United States could be quite useful in eliminating or reducing anxiety, helping you avoid breaking the law, and possibly saving you money.

As we write, the entire structure of United States Customs tariff classifications is being revised. The Tariff Schedules of the United States are about to be replaced by the Harmonized System of Tariff Classifications of the United States which will "harmonize" American tariff classifications with those of its major trading partners. The date of implementation has not yet been determined. Fortunately, for our purposes there will be very few important changes in the customs treatment of works of art.

From the customs perspective, the three scenarios we described above are essentially treated identically. The general rule of thumb is that works of the fine arts are admitted duty-free into the U.S. regardless of the medium used or the age of the work. As you would expect, there are exceptions to this general rule and, among them, some surprises.

The Tariff Schedules specify the following groups of artworks as entitled to enter the U.S. duty-free:

1) paintings, pastels, drawings and sketches, whether originals or not, executed entirely by hand;

2) engravings, etchings, lithographs, woodcuts, and other prints, unbound, and printed by hand from plates, stones or blocks etched, drawn or engraved with hand tools;

3) original sculptures and statuary in any form, from any material, whether in the round, in relief, cut, carved or otherwise wrought by hand or cast but only if it is the production of a professional sculptor. This applies to the first ten castings (the first twelve when the Harmonized System is in effect), replicas or reproductions made from the sculptor's original work or model, with or without a change in scale and whether or not the sculptor is alive at the time the casting, replica or reproduction is made.

4) original mosaics

5) any other original works of the free fine arts, in any media including, but not limited to, applied paper and other materials, manufactured or otherwise, such as are used in collages.

6) works of art produced by American artists residing temporarily abroad.

The categories described above apply only to works by artists; the products of artisans or craftspersons are not included. For paintings, drawings, engravings and the other two dimensional works listed, this generally does not pose a problem because the threshold of skill required for customs purposes is quite low. Nevertheless, reproductions of these same works would not be duty-free if produced by a photochemical or mechanical process.

Problems can and do occur frequently with sculpture. Customs will want to know the identity of the artist, his training in the fine arts and whether his works have been exhibited in museums or galleries. If Customs is unconvinced that the sculptor is an established fine artist, the work may be dutiable.

In addition, no utilitarian works of art are admitted duty-free. This includes, among other categories, jewelry and other items of apparel. Objects made of glass or ceramic, with rare exceptions, will be considered utilitarian. The same is true for other objects which, apart from customs considerations, might be considered sculpture. For example, a carved marble mantlepiece (assuming that it cannot qualify as an antique) is dutiable regardless of the skill of the stone carver or the beauty of the work. Objects produced by artisans will include many works that purchasers will consider to be a works of fine art. An object made in a traditional manner where the artist is not identified will usually be considered by Customs to be made by an artisan, and thus dutiable, despite the level of skill employed.

The Tariff Schedules specifically state that duty-free entry does not apply to architectural, engineering, industrial or commercial drawings or plans; painted or decorated manufactured articles, such as vases, cups and plates; articles made in any part by stenciling, or by photochemical or other mechanical processes. This means that photographs, works of any medium intended for a commercial purpose (such as paintings or drawings for a magazine or brochures), or the architectural renderings of a world famous architect are all dutiable.

Although the tariff schedules specifically provide that works of art by American artists residing temporarily abroad are admitted duty free, the Customs treatment of such works is actually no different than any other works of art entering the United States. In fact, the Harmonized System does not even include a provision for American artists temporarily residing abroad. But this change will have no practical effect on whether an American artist's work is dutiable.

It is often easier to clear customs by carrying the works of art you are intending to import as personal baggage when entering the United States rather than shipping them separately. Usually, if the declared value of the art you are importing (whether it is produced by you or another artist) is below $1000, and the works are accepted as fine art by the customs official, you are likely to be waived through with no further formalities. If the declared value is $1000 or more, or you are importing the works of art as other than personal baggage, then it is more likely that a formal customs entry will be necessary.

A formal entry will often require the posting of a bond and the necessity of producing documents to prove value and possibly the identity of the artist. The latter is particularly true with sculpture. Because of the bond and paperwork requirements, many importers prefer to engage the services of a customs broker who can also arrange for direct delivery of the imported goods.

The customs duty is not paid at the time the works of art are released from customs. Instead, you will later receive a bill from the Customs Service. You have twenty days in which to respond to the amount charged, either by paying the bill or stating why you believe the duty amount is incorrect. If the Customs official in charge of our importation does not change his mind, then the duty assessment is "liquidated," that is, considered final. If you want to pursue the matter, you have ninety days from the date of liquidation to protest the duty assessment. Protests are ordinarily handled by attorneys and take us beyond the scope of this book. Suffice it to say that Customs does not often lose protest cases involving works of art.

The Customs Service attempts to be objective as much as possible. There are nevertheless borderline cases where discretion must be exercised, and sometimes the decision goes against the importer. There are steps you can take to simplify your experiences with Customs. First, you can attempt to obtain a binding ruling on the Customs treatment of your planned imports by writing to: U.S. Customs Service, 1301 Constitution Ave., Washington D.C. 20229, Attention: Binding Rulings. To obtain a binding ruling, you must describe the specific articles to be imported and provide information about the professional status of the artist. Where you are the artist, you would provide your own credentials. A binding ruling guarantees that the customs classification of your imports will not be different at the time of importation from what is stated in the ruling.

Second, if you know the port of entry for your imports, you may contact the Customs import specialist who is responsible for works of art in that region by calling the U.S. Customs Office closest to the port of entry. While that person is not authorized to give a binding ruling, you are likely to get an accurate idea of whether the works of art you are importing will be admitted duty free and, if not, what duty rate is likely to apply.

We have one major word of caution. When you are carrying works of art with you as personal baggage, resist the inclination not to declare them upon your entry into the United States. Failure to declare any article that is imported into the United States and not included within the scope of the personal duty exemption (currently at $400), subjects that article to permanent confiscation by the Customs Service. This applies even if the article were otherwise duty free. The Boston Museum of Fine Arts lost a painting by Raphael as a result of confiscation by Customs after the person carrying the painting into the United States as personal baggage from Europe unwisely chose not to declare it. (The painting was returned to Italy.)

When works of art originally produced in the United States temporarily leave the country for any reason (such as a gallery or museum exhibition overseas), it is important to have some proof that these works were produced in the U.S. Otherwise, when they return to the United States, the works may be dutiable depending upon what customs classification is applied. Contrary to the practice with manufactured goods, works of art cannot be registered with Customs to establish that these objects are U.S. goods being returned. However, under the current law, if the work of art returns to the U.S. with an increase in value such as where the work has been framed, the extra value is likely to be dutiable. Under the Harmonized System, framing would not ordinarily be dutiable.

A final word on antiques and ethnographic works: any antique object that is over 100 years old and any ethnographic piece made in a traditional aboriginal style and over fifty years old is admitted duty free. If substantial repairs of any of these objects were made within three years of importation, the value of the repairs is subject to duty.

IMMIGRATION

For those readers who are not citizens of the United States and either reside outside the United States or are in the United States on temporary visas, some discussion of the immigration laws relating to working and residing in the United States might be helpful. If you are living outside the United States and contemplate travelling to American for any purposes other than tourism, it is very important that you have some understanding of how American immigration law may affect the purpose of your trip. For example, if your goal is to emigrate to the United States for permanent residency or citizenship, it may be a serious error to apply initially for a visitor's visa and expect to change your status once you are in the United States. The reason for this is that the applicant for a nonimmigrant visa must represent that he or she intends to remain only temporarily in the United States. To apply later for permanent residency, following entry into the country, may raise questions regarding possible fraudulent procurement of the nonimmigrant visa.

The immigration laws of the United States distinguish two general classes of visas, immigrant and non-immigrant. There are numerous classifications of non-immigrant visas. The most common and important, and easiest to obtain, are the ordinary visitors' visas of which there are two kinds: business (B-1) and pleasure (B-2). If you are planning to visit the U.S. as a tourist, the B-2 visa is the appropriate one. Of course, this only applies if you need a visa. Visitors from some countries, including Canada, may enter the United States for up to ninety days without a visa. The B-1 visa will enable you to conduct business or engage in professional activities related to your foreign work as long as you do not perform services that are considered local employment in the U.S. You apply for these visas at a U.S. Consulate. To be eligible for a B-1 or B-2 visa you must possess a passport that will be valid for at least six months following the expiration of your visa. In addition, you may be required to demonstrate to the consular officer that you have the means to support yourself during your trip, that you intend to return to your country of residence and, in the case of the business visitor, that you are legitimately engaged in business.

For an artist who wants to travel to the U.S. for business reasons, the B-1 visa can be very useful. In general, a visitor to the United States cannot engage in local employment. American employers are subject to fines (and possible jail terms) for providing employment to aliens who are not properly documented. With the B-1 visa, however, you can engage in many business related activities without violating the local employment restriction. For example, you could attend an opening of an exhibition of your works and travel around the country soliciting commissions, or interesting other galleries in your work. You can give demonstrations or lectures. As a rule of thumb, as long as you are not an employee of anyone in the United States and you do not receive compensation in the United States for your business activities, you are probably not violating the terms of your visa. With a B-1 or B-2 visa you can engage in creating works of art, but, again, you cannot receive compensation in the United States if you seek to sell, trade, lease or otherwise transfer ownership of the artwork.

There are other types of non-immigrant visas for which an artist can apply. A student visa (either F-1 for academic or M-1 for vocational training) is available for temporary stays in the United States, but this type of visa may be more difficult to obtain than a B-1 or B-2 visa. To be eligible for a student visa, you must demonstrate the following:

1. Proof of acceptance into an academic or vocational institution or certain language programs;

2. English language proficiency or enrollment in a course designed to lead to proficiency;

3. Financial resources to cover all expenses for the duration of your education program;

4. Clear intent to leave the United States following completion of the educational program.

Once the student enters the United States and begins a course of study, he must maintain student status or face possible deportation.

Because a student visa is available for vocational as well as academic programs, an artist need not be accepted by a college or university. He may be able to visit the United States and directly further his or her artistic skills by enrolling in an art school. The artist would then apply for the M-1 visa. Besides the training or education received, a student visa may enable the artist to remain in the States for a longer period of time than would otherwise be possible with a tourist visa. However, the M-1 visa is limited to maximum one-year visit. The academic F-1 visa is valid for up to eight years if continuous student status is maintained, and may be renewed for another eight-year period.

For those artists with contacts in the United States who are willing to offer them temporary employment, another possible non-immigrant visa is one of the temporary worker visas: H-1, H-2 or H-3. These visas, like those for students, require more documentation and take longer to obtain than the B-1 or B-2 visas. The H-1 visa is available only for individuals of distinguished merit and ability who come to the United States in a temporary capacity to provide exceptional services which require the outstanding skills of the foreign visitor. There are two ways an applicant can demonstrate distinguished merit and ability: being preeminent in one's field or being a member of a recognized profession.

In addition to the documentation the visa applicant must provide, the prospective employer of the H-1 applicant must file a petition with the Immigration and Naturalization Service (INS) to support the application for the H-1 visa. The period of services requested in the petition cannot exceed three years. The visa applicant must also demonstrate that he intends to leave the United States after completing the work covered by the visa, and that he has a foreign residence to which he intends to return.

The distinguished merit and ability requirement probably limits the availability of this visa to artists who have well established reputations. For those artists who may not be sufficiently well known for the H-1 visa, there are two additional H-category visas, the H-2B and H-3 visas. Both of these visas, particularly the H-3, may be difficult to obtain for visual arts-related purposes.

The H-2B visa is available to an applicant for the purpose of providing temporary services in the United States only when unemployed qualified American citizens or permanent residents cannot be found to do the job. The employer must demonstrate that the need for the visa applicant is only temporary. (For example, the owner of a pricey retail clothing store might need an artist skilled in *trompe l'oeil* to paint an interior wall. Once the wall is completed the storeowner would have no further need of the artist's services.) The employer must also file a petition on behalf of the person seeking the H-2B visa, and the petition must be accompanied by a certification from the U.S. Department of Labor that no United States workers are available for the job. Considering the number of artists in the United States, it may be difficult to obtain a certification that there are no unemployed and qualified American artists to satisfy an employer's need for temporary visual arts-related services, unless the foreign artist is specially suited for the job.

The H-3 visa applies only to trainee positions with an American employer. The training theoretically can be in any area including the arts. Documents required to apply for this visa include a petition by the U.S. employer which must include a detailed description of the training program, the reasons the employer is willing to provide the training and the expected benefits to the trainee. The visa holder is not permitted to engage in productive employment while in the U.S. under this visa. Although there is no prescribed limit for the duration of an H-3 visa, it can only be valid for the length of the training program. Overall, there are probably few opportunities for a foreign artist to find an American business that is willing to provide a training program that would qualify under the H-3 requirements.

For an artist, a more attractive prospect that the H-visa is the Exchange Visitor J-1 visa. The purpose behind this visa is to promote international relations between the United States and other countries by providing training which the visa holder can utilize in his own country. The J-1 visa is available only to participants in certain programs that are approved by the United States Information Agency (USIA). A large variety of training programs, including those that are arts-related, are eligible for USIA approval. Any American government or private organization or agency is eligible to apply for a designation as an Exchange Visitor Program. If the designation is granted by the USIA, the organization can then provide the necessary forms to the J-1 visa applicant.

Let's assume that you have located an Exchange Program that satisfies your interests, and the Program is willing to extend an invitation to you. You must then take into consideration the limitations of the J-1 visa. Although there are no set time limits for the validity of a J-1 visa, the duration of the visa is generally limited to the length of the training program. The foreign visitor must maintain his status as a full-time participant in the program for the entire period he remains in the United States under the visa.

Probably the most severe limitation under the J-1 visa is the requirement that under certain circumstances a visa holder must return to his home country for a minimum of two years before being eligible to apply for an immigrant visa, permanent residency or a non-immigrant H-type visa.

The two-year foreign residency requirement applies to three groups of exchange program participants, only two of which might reasonably relate to artists:

1. Where the exchange program is wholly or partially funded by the United States government, by the government of the exchange visitor's nationality or last legal residence, or by an international agency whose funding is contributed to by the U.S. government or the government of the exchange visitor's last legal residence;

2. Where the exchange visitor's fields of knowledge and skills appear on the Exchange Visitor's Skills list. This list, which is developed and published by the U.S. Secretary of State, reflects the areas of expertise individual countries consider to be of major importance.

It would be relatively easy for a J-1 visa applicant to determine whether one or both of these circumstances apply. The program should know the source of its funding and the Exchange Visitor Skills List should be available from any U.S. Consulate. If neither of the two circumstances described above apply, then the visa holder would not be affected by the foreign residence requirement.

If the two-year foreign residence requirement otherwise applies, the only way to avoid having to leave the United States is by obtaining a waiver. There are several reasons for which a waiver might be available. These include exceptional hardship (generally involving a United States citizen, spouse or child), anticipated persecution in the country to which the foreign visitor would return, submission of a "no objection" statement by the visa holder's country of nationality or last legal residence, and requests by interested U.S. government agencies.

Generally, a foreign visitor who enters the United States on one non-immigrant visa may apply for a different non-immigrant visa while in the United States. One major exception, as we described above, is the J-1 visa holder who must comply with the two-year foreign residency requirement.

There is, of course, the possibility that an artist from another country might be interested in obtaining permanent residence in the United States. This aspect of immigration law is quite complex and is beyond the scope of this book. Speaking very generally, however, unless an artist desiring to immigrate to the United States has a close family relationship to either an American citizen or a lawful permanent resident of the U.S., or can establish that he has "exceptional ability" as an artist, the quota requirement for individual countries may result in a wait of several years before an application will be processed.

We have given you a very simplified and selective overview of the various visas available from the United States government for the purpose of visiting or emigrating to the U.S. Obtaining a visa other than the B-1 and B-2 visitor's visas can be a complicated and frustrating experience. If you are an artist contemplating applying for anything other than a visitor's visa, we urge you to consult with someone who has expertise in American immigration law, preferably an American attorney who specializes in that area of practice. It is important to keep in mind that the decision to grant a visa, even a regular B-2 tourist visa, is completely at the discretion of the U.S. Consular officer. Therefore, be prepared when you make your application.

9

GETTING
LEGAL HELP

The information in the preceding chapters is basic and will prepare an artist for consultation with an attorney or another professional. It is intended to be preventive advice. This chapter includes more practical information about obtaining legal help, what to do in a legal crisis, how to be prepared for one and some basics about the artist as a manufacturer.

LAWYERS

"Pro bono" legal services are those offered free of charge to people or entities which cannot afford to pay for them. Some legal insurance programs exist but they are rare. Most people must pay dearly for legal services and therefore may have difficulty affording good legal advice. The following list includes organizations of lawyers around the United States dedicated to providing legal help to artists, including free or low-fee services. If these locations are not convenient or these agencies do not prove satisfactory, call the local (state or city) bar association to ask for a referral to a lawyer. Many lawyers will provide a small amount of free advice to anyone needing help and a free referral to someone who will do the whole job for free. In addition to offering legal referrals, the organizations listed below sponsor lectures and workshops and give some over-the-counter help.

California Lawyers for the Arts
Fort Mason Center, Building C
San Francisco, CA 94123
415-775-7200

Colorado Lawyers for the Arts
P. O. Box 30428
Denver, CO 80203
303-830-0379

Connecticut Volunteer Lawyers
  for the Arts
190 Trumbull Street
Hartford, CT 06103
203-566-4770

Georgia Volunteer Lawyers
  for the Arts
P.O. Box 1131
Atlanta, GA 30301-1131
404-586-4945

Lawyers and Accountants for the
  Arts
The Artists Foundation Inc.
8 Park Plaza
Boston, MA 02116
617-227-2787

Lawyers for the Creative Arts
623 South Wabash Avenue,
  Suite 201
Chicago, IL 60605
312-427-1800

Philadelphia Volunteer Lawyers for
  the Arts
251 South 18th Street
Philadelphia, PA 19103
215-545-3385

Volunteer Lawyers for the Arts
1285 Avenue of the Americas,
  3rd Floor
New York, NY 10019
212-977-9270

Washington Area Lawyers for
  the Arts
2025 I Street N.W., Suite 1114
Washington, D.C. 20006
202-861-0055

State and local bar associations for arts committees are also located in many states and cities, including the following:

Florida
Iowa
Kansas
Kentucky
Maine
Rhode Island

Maryland (Baltimore)
Minnesota (Minneapolis)
Missouri (St. Louis)
Montana (Missoula)
New Jersey (Trenton)
North Carolina (Raleigh)

Ohio (Cleveland)   Utah (Salt Lake City)
South Carolina (Greenville)   Washington (Seattle)
Texas (Austin)

Like most professionals, lawyers specialize. Some attorneys specialize in tax matters, some in family law, others in criminal law. Analyze the problem as closely as possible before seeking help; then ask for specialized help. Never hesitate to call the state bar association to check up on the lawyer recommended, to learn whether he is licensed and in good standing. No lawyer may take on a client's case if doing so will cause a conflict of interest with another client's matter; so be aware of that potential problem, particularly with a large law firm that has many clients. Also, expect to pay the out-of-pocket expenses which the lawyer incurs in the representation, even if he is willing to forego billing for his time.

RESOURCES

Books are available to help artists. Most of the offices noted above maintain libraries which the public may use. In addition to books such as this one, large bookstores carry the many do-it-yourself legal books which include the information and forms a person may need to form a corporation, write a will, or get a divorce. These are helpful for simple situations, even if an attorney is hired, because they help the client to organize his plans before consulting the attorney and thus save money.

Forms are available at stationery stores for many types of documents, including leases, powers of attorney, wills, trusts, sales of property, deeds, bills of sale for personal property, etc. These cost very little and can be used in uncomplicated transactions just by filling in the blanks, although notarization or other formalities may be required. As with do-it-yourself books and kits, great caution should be exercised before casually preparing legal documents without the advice of an attorney.

Court and other government clerks offer forms and when they are not too busy such people will often give free over-the-counter assistance, particularly on procedure. Public libraries often maintain law books. A good reference librarian can often be an excellent source of simple legal help. Directories of lawyers are available at public libraries and court libraries.

In trying to solve your own legal problems, remember to talk to the staff of the government agency involved or with jurisdiction over the subject matter in general. As stated above, all major offices of the IRS offer telephone and in-person assistance. Federal, state and local government offices (usually listed in the government pages of the telephone directory) answer calls and letters from the public every day except weekends and legal holidays. If you want to read a particular law or regulation, go to the agency that administers it. Most documents written by or filed with the government are public records and therefore available to anyone to read or copy. Most agencies publish free digests explaining the laws they administer in lay terms. The United States government, which has its own bookstores selling its publications, publishes a wide range of information on many subjects.

Some agencies are established to provide consumer protection. If the legal problem arises from some potential abuse by a lender, vendor, landlord or employer, check in the front of the telephone directory for the name of an agency which appears to regulate such conduct. You may discover that it is a legal necessity to file certain documents or demands with an agency immediately after the problem occurs.

BE PREPARED

Not everyone can follow all the preventive advice in the preceding chapters all the time. It is best to keep written records of transactions and events, no matter how ordinary the circumstances. Even a daily journal with handwritten notes may suffice. In a legal crisis, almost inevitably people are forced to remember what happened in the past. If their records are poor but they sense trouble brewing, they should start that minute to keep notes. It is never too late to begin keeping records. Written notes may be used in depositions or on the witness stand when the person testifying cannot recall what actually happened.

Similarly, keep papers together in an organized manner and take valuable papers to a safety deposit box. This may seem obvious or even ridiculous. In an IRS audit, however, the burden of proof is on the taxpayer to establish what amounts of money were spent on what activities. If you are audited and you cannot find your cancelled checks or credit card receipts to prove expenditures, you could face a large tax obligation that might have been avoided. If your studio burns down but you have kept in your safety deposit box a photograph of each work of art in the studio, you will have little difficulty establishing your losses for the insurance adjuster. Keep a copy of your update inventory in your safety deposit box, also.

IF YOU ARE SUED

Civil lawsuits begin procedurally with the filing of a petition or complaint at the court by the plaintiff. The plaintiff must serve a copy of the document on the defendant. This can be done by simply mailing the document to the defendant, by having a process server deliver it, or by having the sheriff do so. If you receive a summons, the procedure generally requires you to file an answer with the court within a certain number of days or else obtain the permission of the court or the opposing party to have more time to do so. Failure to do this simple act may amount to an admission of all the plaintiff's claims and may cost you the lawsuit. For these reasons, if you are sued, you should immediately obtain the assistance of an attorney. It is a good idea to cease communicating with the plaintiff until you have the advice of a lawyer because of the possibility of prejudicing the case. Settlement negotiations must be handled carefully for the same reason.

IF YOU MUST SUE SOMEONE

A lawsuit should always be your last resort for resolving a problem. Not only are lawsuits quite expensive to undertake, they can also destroy relationships. You might argue that where a lawsuit appears necessary there is no relationship worth saving. While this may be true and artists may receive more than their fair share of mistreatment, many disputes, even bitter ones, arise out of genuine disagreement about rights and obligations. In those cases, a relationship worth saving probably exists. The mere fact that you might find free legal services available to you should not encourage you to use the power of the courts to resolve problems. In fact, the courts will often reject and even punish a party bringing "frivolous" litigation.

ARBITRATION

There are useful alternatives to litigation. As stated above, be prepared by having a chronology of events, possibly even a written narrative of what happened. You may find that you can be your own best lawyer by presenting your case to your opponent. Other means of dispute resolution are available also, such as formal and informal arbitration or mediation. The distinction between arbitration and mediation is not always clear. In general, however, mediation involves the mutual agreement of the parties to bring in a neutral third party to help resolve the dispute. Arbitration generally involves a neutral third party acting as a judge. The arbitrator decides who "wins" and what he wins. Often arbitration decisions are binding, i.e., may not be challenged in court except in special circumstances. Both arbitration and mediation may be less expensive and less time consuming than litigation. Arbitrators and mediators charge a small fee, and some arts organizations such as California Lawyers for the Arts assist in providing such services specifically for artists.

Arbitration may actually be required by the terms of an agreement which lies at the root of the dispute. If so, it is extremely difficult and in fact nearly impossible to litigate in court rather than arbitrate before an arbitrator. The rules which the arbitrator must follow should be specified in the original contract between the parties. This is particularly important in view of the understandable but somewhat naive expectation of most parties that arbitration will be handled just as litigation in court. This is not the case unless the parties have so specified. Arbitration proceedings, unless limited by the parties in their contract, can take into consideration a far wider range of evidence and the final decision of the arbitrator may be based on what he perceives the equities of the situation to be. He need not follow the strict letter of the law in making his award.

SMALL CLAIMS COURT

Small Claims Court provides a forum for litigation of disputes involving relatively small amounts of money. Each state sets a different dollar limit for small claims court jurisdiction. States also differ on the permissibility of attorneys representing clients in small claims court. If you plan to sue someone in small claims court but the defendant plans to defend himself with an attorney in court, consider the possibility that you may be outmaneuvered by the attorney on the other side of the case. Even in states where no attorney representation is permitted in court, a party to a small claims court suit may nevertheless hire a lawyer to advise him on preparing his case. Generally, people do not do so because the cost of the attorney may be more than the value of the case. A defendant who has been sued in small claims court may use an attorney because of precedential or other nonmonetary value of the case. Also, in many states, by countersuing the plaintiff for more money than the small claims court allows or by using some other procedural tactic, a defendant may have the case removed to the trial court where attorneys are permitted. In any case, small claims court judgments are binding just as those by courts of higher jurisdiction.

No matter what means of dispute resolution you elect, be careful to file your claim with the court or appropriate authority before the expiration of the statute of limitations. The statute of limitations is a time bar for stale claims. It generally runs from one to ten years, depending upon the nature of the claim and the state law. Once the statute expires, you may not sue the other party. Similarly, be careful to check on "jurisdictional prerequisites," which are legal requirements that you first file your claim with some special agency having jurisdiction over the particular type of complaint you have. For example, if you wish to sue your boss for sex discrimination, you may first be required to file a claim with your state civil rights commission. Jurisdictional filing prerequisites often have very short deadlines, sometimes as little as a few months. Failure to observe this formality can cost you the lawsuit.

LEGAL REMEDIES

Depending upon the problem, a wide range of remedies are available for an injured person who prosecutes a claim. If another party is engaged or about to engage in a clear wrong, such as infringement of a copyright, for which no other remedy is adequate, a court may issue an injunction preventing or ordering the defendant to cease his activity. If, however, the defendant's actions have ceased and the court can award money damages to the plaintiff to give him the benefit of the bargain in the contract or to compensate him for his injury in a tort case (a civil wrong not arising out of a contract), then the court will generally do so rather than issue an injunction.

Courts will very rarely fashion a remedy compelling a person to perform personal services, even if the person previously agreed to do so. Instead, courts prefer money damages. For example, if Guido and Mrs. Patron sign a contract whereby Guido agrees to paint Mrs. Patron's portrait but Guido refuses to do so, a court probably will not order him to paint the portrait. Instead, Guido may be ordered to repay Mrs. Patron any money she spent in making arrangements for the portrait; if hiring another artist to paint the portrait costs her $1,000 more, a court might order Guido to pay her that amount, also. Guido is not likely to be compelled to perform a personal service, however.

10
PRACTICAL CONSIDERATIONS

THE ARTIST AS MANUFACTURER

A professional artist is a fabricator and a vendor of goods. Although the law regards some element of his output as labor, generally the final product is treated as goods and the artist as the manufacturer. As such, the artist and his workshop must comply with many of the laws which regulate manufacturing and selling merchandise, for example the zoning ordinances governing the neighborhood in which the workshop is located.

Environmental laws in most states, particularly large commercial states such as New York, California and Illinois, require special permits for many manufacturing activities. Three activities often requiring environmental permits are operating a source of air pollutants, generating, transporting or disposing of hazardous waste, and releasing pollutants to a source of drinking water. Generally, threshold amounts of pollutants must be involved before permits are required. An artist should contact his state and local health department officials for detailed information about environmental laws and permits.

Employers must observe the restrictions of federal, state and local labor and worker-safety laws. Usually, a minimum number of employees triggers such requirements as proper working environment, safety equipment and accessible rest areas. Discrimination against persons on the basis of sex, race, age, handicap and veteran status are illegal. Employees also have the right to organize into unions without harassment by their employer. Regardless of the number of employees, federal and state employer tax laws requiring social security payments and the withholding of income tax must be observed.

Extremely important, is the artist's continuing liability for the manufactured quality (as opposed to the aesthetic quality) of his product. Artwork is "goods" within the meaning of the Uniform Commercial Code. As such, artworks are sold together with express and implied warranties by their sellers. These warranties are:

1. The express warranty that the goods are what the seller describes them as being

2. The implied warranty of merchantability, i.e. that the artwork is not defective

3. The implied warranty of fitness for a particular purpose which arises when the artist knows the buyer's purpose for the goods, when the artist knows the buyer is relying on the artist's skill, and the buyer actually does so.

Numerous cases have arisen over whether the UCC governs sales from parties such as artists to parties such as galleries. Suffice it to say that an artist regularly engaged in selling his own works to anyone should be careful to avoid breaching these warranties. The problem of inherent vice (a built-in material defect) in artwork would generate a lawsuit against the artist seller under these warranties, particularly in the case of a commissioned work. Although the warranty of merchantability may be disclaimed if done so carefully, the UCC can form the basis of a lawsuit against an artist whose work deteriorates.

Tort liability is also a major concern for artists whose works could somehow cause injury to those who come into contact with them. An artist whose product injures another party may find that he is sued for negligence by the injured party. The best prevention is extreme care in production and handling. Insurance against such claims is also advisable, to protect the artist from personal liability. Insurance can be difficult to obtain and expensive, however.

Sometime's an artist's own property is damaged by others, for example when an object is damaged in shipping. In such a situation, the artist may be able to demand that the party at fault pay the cost of repairs or, in the case of a total loss, reimburse the artist for the value of the lost object. The artist who carries insurance on his works may be able to collect these amounts from his own insurer who will then seek a remedy from the party at fault. If no insurance is available and the damage is great, the artist may have to resort to a lawsuit to collect this amount. In all cases, careful packing and moving are necessary for fragile objects or the artist himself may be found to be partly negligent and therefore unable to collect the full amount of the loss from the other party.

INSURANCE

The extent of an artist's need to maintain insurance depends primarily upon his working and living arrangements. An insurance policy is essentially a contract in which the insured party agrees to pay the insurance company a specific sum, known as a premium, in exchange for a specified maximum amount of coverage for specific risks of loss. Generally, an artist would be concerned about two types of risks—property-related risks and liability risks. Property insurance will protect you against loss to your own property, such as is caused by fire and theft. Liability insurance will protect you against claims made against you by a third party such as a claim for personal injury or damage to the third party's property.

Many renters and most homeowners maintain some amount of insurance covering both their dwelling and its contents. Many artists may resist the idea of paying for insurance to cover their personal possessions.

Yet, for artists who live and work on the same premises, and who keep their inventories in the same locations, insurance policies may make good business sense. The same is true for artists who have studios in locations different from their dwellings. For artists who depend to some degree on income derived from sales of the artwork, a loss of inventory can wipe out many months of creative effort and corresponding income.

It is very important to comply with the terms of any insurance policy you obtain. It is a contract. For example, assuming you are able to purchase a policy covering your ongoing artistic production, you will probably be required to present some documentary proof regarding specific losses you incur. Photographs of the pieces which have been stolen, lost or damaged will assist you in proving what losses you have sustained. The monetary value of the loss will be determined by means of some type of appraisal. If you have already been selling your work actively, it will be much easier to establish a market value for losses of inventory that you may incur. You also will be required to give prompt notice to the insurance company if you experience a loss. Some policies require fire and smoke prevention equipment, special locks, etc., where valuable works of art are stored.

The second type of insurance, liability insurance, can be very important under certain circumstances. For instance, if you are a sculptor like Skeezix D. whose work is frequently large-scale and located in public spaces, there is the potential for personal injury claims resulting from contact between the public and your work. Frequently, work of this nature is commissioned. It is very important to have a clear understanding about who has the obligation to maintain the liability insurance in connection with the installation and permanent exhibition of the work. Keep in mind that the construction phase of some work also carries risk of personal injury, against which you are also advised to maintain insurance.

Where you have a relationship with an art dealer, you should have as part of your agreement with him an express understanding about who bears the risk of loss in connection with the transportation, exhibition or storage of your work. If the dealer agrees to do so, you should be sure that he either currently has insurance to cover such risks or that he will purchase insurance prior to receiving your pieces. Where you decide to purchase your own insurance, whether property or liability coverage, you will do well to be very thorough with your insurance broker about the types of risks for which you seek coverage. Otherwise, at the time of a loss, you may discover to your dismay that your policy does not provide coverage. Also, it is essential to be truthful with the insurance company representative both at the time the policy application is filled out and at the time of making a claim. If there is any suspicion of fraud, the insurance company may very well deny your claim and cancel your policy. Under those circumstances, you may find that it is difficult to obtain replacement insurance.

COMMISSIONS

For some artists, commissions can be a reliable source of income and creative satisfaction. For others, commissions can be major headaches with little or no financial return. If you keep in mind that commissions are contracts, you will prepare yourself for dealing effectively with the business aspects of the commission. (See Chapter 2 on contracts.) Besides the major terms such as price, subject, medium, size and timing, there is the question of whether the artist will guarantee the other party's satisfaction with the piece. Courts often enforce a "satisfaction guaranteed" provision in a commission contract.

If you are not prepared to risk the possibility that the commissioning party will reject your work, do not accept the commission on those terms, or at least build in some protection for yourself. For example, in exchange for the patron's right to reject the work ultimately, you might require that he compensate you for materials and time at a specific hourly rate. Where "satisfaction guaranteed" is not part of the deal, you can decide how much specificity regarding the final product you are willing to accept in the agreement. The more specific the description, the less creative freedom you will have and the more opportunity the patron will have to argue that you did not comply precisely with the terms of the contract.

As a final suggestion, have a look at the sample commission contract in the Appendix.

THE BERNE CONVENTION

A total of 76 countries are signatories to the Berne Convention, including the U.K., France, Italy, East and West Germany, Switzerland, Canada, Japan, Sweden, Spain, Portugal, New Zealand, Australia, and Liechtenstein. Most of the same countries are also signatories to the Universal Copyright Convention. Note, however, that the U.S.S.R. has signed the latter but not the Berne Convention.

Determining the extent of and requirements for protection of an author's or artist's copyright interests under the Berne Convention is complicated by the fact that there are various amendments to the treaty and not every nation that is a signatory to the treaty has bound itself to the most recent version. If you are considering publication in a Berne convention country, you should consult legal counsel for the most recent information on a specific country's Berne obligations. In lieu of consulting an attorney, you can obtain useful, but not as current, information from a specialized publication such as *Nimmer on Copyright*.

APPENDIX

The following pages contain a sample Artist/Dealer Agreement. This form is provided courtesy of California Lawyers for the Arts. This is merely one type of Artist/Dealer Agreement, and it is not intended to be applicable to all situations.

ARTIST-DEALER AGREEMENT

This agreement is between:

NAME: _____ (ARTIST)

ADDRESS: _____

city   state   zip

TELEPHONE: (   ) _____

and _____ hereinafter referred to as "the Dealer."

The terms of this agreement are as follows:

1. <u>Limited, exclusive agency</u>. Artist hereby appoints Dealer his sole and exclusive agent for the sale of his/her works of art in the following geographical area.

_____

Any exceptions in reference to works being shown and/or displayed in other outlets in this geographical territory must be in the form of a *written* agreement which must be signed by both Artist and Dealer prior to any works being exhibited for sale.

2. <u>Creation, Title and Receipt</u>. The Dealer acknowledges receipt of each piece of art as a "bona fide" example of the works of a particular artist and agrees that all work furnished to him shall be represented as such.

3. <u>Duration of Agreement</u>. This agreement shall become effective upon the date of signing and shall continue in effect until _____ 19____, at which time the agreement may be rewritten for another time period. This agreement may be terminated by either party giving 30 days written notice of that party's intent to terminate.

4. COVENANTS AND PROMISES OF THE DEALER

The Dealer hereby covenants, promises, represents, agrees and acknowledges as follows:

(A). To receive on consignment the art works of the Artist:

(B). To make reasonable and bona fide efforts to sell each said art work consigned to the Dealer by the Artist and in any event at a price not less than that agreed upon in writing unless authorized by the Artist. If an art work is sold, the gallery shall receive 50% of the sales price set forth in writing. The remaining 50% shall be paid to the artist.

(C). To exercise all due and reasonable care in the handling, storage and temporary delivery to other persons of said art works until returned to the possession of the Artist. The Dealer also agrees to provide insurance on all the Artist's works covering such losses as theft, loss or damage from any source or cause whatsoever while the said art works are in the possession of the Dealer, left on approval with or rented to a prospective customer. The required insurance shall be in an amount not less than the full value of the works covered by this agreement less the Dealer's commission.

(D). To deliver to the Artist on or before the end of every quarter during the effectiveness of this agreement, a full and complete statement of the inventory and account and setting forth the following:

1. the particular art works sold (or rented)
2. the date of sale or rental, the amount and the terms thereof:
3. the names and addresses of the purchasers to whom the particular works have been sold or rented; and
4. the location of unsold works not on the premises of the gallery.

The Dealer represents that said statement shall be accurate and complete in all respects. The Artist shall have the right and shall receive at the end of the fiscal year (December 31st) a 1099 FORM which will state the total sales for the year.

(E). To remit to the Artist within 14 days from the receipt of payment full payment due to the Artist. If the Artist has agreed to installment payments by the purchaser, then the Dealer agrees to remit to the Artist his/her share of each installment payment. Any and all reasonable effort will be made to verify the credit of each client. Losses due to failure of a client's credit will be shared equally by the Dealer and the Artist.

(F). To rent the artwork, if the Dealer believes it to be a necessary inducement to the sale of an Artist's work for a period not to exceed 3 months, unless consent to a longer period has been given by the Artist. Rental fees shall be divided as follows: 50% to the Artist and 50% to the Dealer, in accordance with paragraph E. In the event that the work is sold, the amount of the rental fees shall be deducted from the Artist's price and the Dealer's profit.

5. Conditions of sales:

(A). Purchaser will, within reason, allow purchased works to be borrowed for the purpose of museum and retrospective exhibits.

(B). That Dealer will not allow any of the works to be copied, photographed or reproduced except for the purpose of appearing in a catalog or advertisement of the Artist's work or with the prior written consent of the Artist.

(C). That Dealer will have printed in a prominent place on each bill of sale the following legend: "The right to copy, photograph or reproduce the works of art identified herein is reserved by the Artist."

(D). Nothwithstanding the foregoing, reproduction rights may be specifically sold by Dealer with the Artist's written consent. Dealer shall not receive any commissions on royalties or sales of reproduction rights unless Dealer has sold or arranged for same, in which Dealer's commission shall be 20% of the fee received by Artist.

6. Full Promotion of Artist:

(A). Dealer agrees to promote artist and to insure that all reasonable effort is put into the promotion and sales of Artist's works of art not only within the aforementioned LIMITED, EXCLUSIVE AGENCY portion of this agreement but also to make known to Artist other potential outlets in other geographical areas. Dealer also agrees to write a letter of recommendation for Artist whenever desired by Artist.

(B). Dealer also agrees to enter print and painting competitions for Artist and to furnish to Artist at his request a list of all forthcoming competitions. Should Artist win a cash prize or purchase award from competitions that Dealer may enter for Artist, Dealer agrees to remit 95% of all purchase award money and to retain 5% to help defray expenses.

7. COVENANTS AND PROMISES OF THE ARTIST
The Artist hereby covenants, promises, represents and agrees as follows:

(A). To authorize the Dealer during the period of this agreement to deliver title to the art works covered by this agreement to purchasers and to collect from them a price not less than the minimum price set forth for that work in writing.

(B). To deliver on consignment art works created and owned by the Artist for purposes of sale and display. During the period of acceptance of this agreement the Artist agrees to forebear from making any agreements to sell or transfer at any time art works already assigned to the Dealer, without the Dealer's written consent and to forbear from selling and consigning, without the consent in writing works produced by him/her to any other agent. If such a sale should occur, the Dealer shall receive 20% of the selling price.

(C). To give the Dealer authority to modify the selling price agreed upon by the Artist by up to 10%.

(D). To accept delivery of and/or remove consigned art pieces not sold at the end of the consignment period if so requested by the Dealer and to remove at any time works on the premises of the Dealer within 30 days of receipt of written request from the Dealer.

(E). To bear the costs of transporting works from the Artist's studio to the Dealer unless other arrangements are made in writing.

(F). To furnish and provide new images as they are available and to supply replacement works (if available in the case of multiples) and to keep dealer informed of images remaining in the edition in cases of multiple images.

(G). To maintain a current biography (vita) on the premises of the Dealer. Dealer also agrees to assist in compilation of biography (vita) of Artist if so asked. Dealer also agrees to furnish to the Artist copies of any press clippings, news releases and other promotional material of interest to the Artist.

8. ARBITRATION CLAUSE

All disputes arising out of this agreement shall be submitted to final and binding arbitration. The arbitrator shall be selected in accordance with the rules of Arts Arbitration and Mediation Services, a program of California Lawyers for the Arts. If such service is not available, the dispute shall be submitted to arbitration in accordance with the laws of California. The arbitrator's award shall be final, and judgment may be entered upon it by any court having jurisdiction thereof.

9.

THIS WRITTEN AGREEMENT is the sole and entire agreement between the parties and shall supercede any and all other agreements between the parties. The parties acknowledge that neither of them has made any representations except those specifically set forth herein and that they have relied on their own judgment in entering into the same.

IN WITNESS THEREOF, the parties hereto have executed this Agreement on the date stated below:

Agreed: _____   Date: _____

Artist

_____   Date: _____

Dealer

The following pages contain a sample Agreement to Fabricate, Transport, and Install a Work of Art. This form is provided courtesy of the Art in Public Places Program of the Arts Commission of San Francisco.

AGREEMENT

to

FABRICATE, TRANSPORT AND INSTALL A WORK OF ART

AT _____

The parties to this agreement are the City of _____, acting by and through its Art Commission ("Commission") and _____ ("Artist"). For the convenience of the parties, this agreement is dated _____.

RECITALS

A. Pursuant to Section _____ of the City Code, the City has allocated funds for acquisition of works of art to adorn the _____ [Building] and authorized the Commission to supervise and control the expenditures for these works.

B. The Commission has appointed a Joint Committee, ["Committee"] to research and recommend artists to produce works of art for the [Building].

C. City Code Section _____ requires that the Commission approve a design or model of a work of art for a specific location before a contract is let for the work.

D. Pursuant to an agreement between the City and the Artist dated _____, 198____, the Artist submitted a proposal for a work of art for a specific location at the [Building] to the Committee.

E. The Committee approved the Artist's maquette and recommended that the Commission enter into an agreement with the Artist for the work if the work as described in the remaining components of the proposal to be submitted to the Commission by the Artist pursuant to the terms of the _____, 198____ agreement ["Proposal"] are first approved by the Committee.

F. The Commission, by resolution number _____, accepted the Committee's recommendation and authorized its Director to enter into this agreement with the Artist for fabrication, transportation and installation of the work in the proposed location at the [Building] on the terms which follow if the Proposal is approved by the Committee.

G. On _____, the Committee approved the Artist's Proposal.

TERMS OF AGREEMENT

1. Scope of Artist's Services.

(a) Fabrication, Transportation and Installation. The Artist shall fabricate the work of art, or cause it to be fabricated, in conformity with the Proposal approved by the Committee and the following specifications:

Dimensions _____

Materials _____

Support or Base _____

Estimated Weight of Work with Base _____

This work shall be entitled _____.

The work shall not deviate in size, design or material from the Proposal and the foregoing specifications unless the change is approved by resolution of the Commission. The Artist is also responsible for transportation of the work to, and installation of the work at the site specified in Paragraph 2 and for all of the expenses associated with fabrication, transportation and installation of the work.

(b) Consultation and Deviations from Proposal. The goal of the parties is a work which represents the creative talents of the Artist and satisfies the specifications set forth in Appendix A to the agreement for the Proposal, which is incorporated herein by reference. The parties recognize that they must consult closely during fabrication and installation of the work in order to accomplish these goals and that changes in the design may become desirable as the work is fabricated. However, the work may not deviate from the Proposal and the specifications set forth in subparagraph (a) unless the deviation is approved by resolution of the Commission. Conformance of the work with the terms set forth in subparagraph (a) is an essential element of this agreement.

2. **Plans for Installation and Identification of Subcontractor.**

   (a) Plans for Installation. No later than _____, 198____, the Artist shall submit to the Commission plans for installation of the work prepared by a structural engineer licensed by the state of _____ and conforming to Uniform Building Code requirements.

   (b) Fabrication by Subcontractor. If the work will be fabricated by a subcontractor, the Artist shall provide the Commission with the name, address and telephone number of the subcontractor not later than _____.

3. **Fabrication and Installation.**

   (a) Schedule for Fabrication and Installation. The Artist shall complete fabrication of the work no later than _____. No later than _____, the Commission shall designate a two week period in which the work shall be installed. The Artist shall give the Commission no less than 15 days notice of the day installation of the work is to begin. Timely fabrication and installation of the work is an essential element of this agreement.

   (b) Review of Work. The Committee and the Commission shall be given access to the work during reasonable business hours in order to review the work and the Artist's progress with fabrication of it.

   (c) Reports on Fabrication and Installation. The Artist shall submit written reports to the Commission no later than _____, describing (1) the fabrication process and (2) the details involved in installation of the work. The report on fabrication shall include the names of any assistants who are responsible for major portions of the fabrication process. The report shall be accompanied by photographs or slides showing the fabrication process and substantiating that the fabrication process has been completed. The report on installation shall include plans for installation and a description of any activities which will have to be coordinated with either the Artist's subcontractors or City personnel or contractors.

   (d) Determination that Work Conform to Proposal. Recognizing the expenses involved in transporting and installing a large work, if requested to do so by the Artist the Commission will, where the Commission deems it feasible, review the work prior to installation and determine by resolution whether it conforms to the terms set forth in subparagraph 1(a).

(e) Storage and Insurance. If the period designated by the Commission for installation of the work begins later than _____, the City will be responsible for the reasonable cost of storing and insuring the work until the period for installation.

(f) Site, Site Preparation, and Access. The Artist shall install the completed work at the [Building] described in Appendix A to the agreement for a Proposal [site]. The City shall provide the site broom clean and free of obstructions. Any other preparation of the site is the responsibility of the Artist.

(g) Arrangements for Access. Arrangements for access to the site for installation must be made through the Commission and access shall not be scheduled until the Commission has received a certificate evidencing liability insurance as required by paragraph 9. Access to the site may be scheduled to avoid interference with normal use of the area. The Artist shall provide the Commission with a written list of the workers, vehicles and equipment which will be involved in the installation of the work at least 15 days in advance of installation so that permits can be issued and security and unloading arrangements made. Cost for vehicle parking shall be the responsibility of the Artist.

(h) Structural Requirements. The Artist shall consult with the project architects to determine as early as possible whether a base or footing, or any other type of structural support, is required for installation of the work. Unless the Commission agrees in writing to the contrary, the Artist is responsible for the cost and installation of any structural support required especially for the work.

4. Disposition of Maquette. The maquette (which is part of the Proposal) shall remain with the Commission until the work is installed and finally accepted by the Commission, except that the Commission may permit the Artist to borrow the maquette if the Artist supplies the Commission with accurate photographs of the maquette as specified by the Commission. The maquette will be returned to the Artist after the work is finally accepted by the City if the Artist provides the City with one 35-mm slide of the maquette, accurate in color and detail, and one 8″ × 10″ glossy, black and white photograph of the maquette.

5. Fee and Interim Payments.

(a) Fee. The Artist's fee for fabrication, transportation and installation of the work, including all expenses relating thereto, whether or not identified in the itemization of expenses included in the Proposal, is $_____. (U.S.) The fee is due and payable by the City when the work is finally accepted by the Commission and an invoice submitted by the Artist.

(b) Interim Payments. The City is not obligated to pay any part of the Artist's fee unless and until the work is finally accepted by the Commission. The City will, however, make payments to the Artist against the fee to assist the Artist with financing the execution, transportation and installation of the work. The amount of the payments is based on the Artist's documented need and shall be made as follows:

(i) Upon contract certification and submission of a request for payment: $_____. [Unless specifically approved by resolution of the Commission, this amount may not exceed 35% of the fee.]

(ii) Following (A) the Commission's determination that fabrication of the work in studio has been completed, (B) submission of the Artist's reports on fabrication and installation of the work, (C) review and approval of the work by authorized representatives of the Commission, (D) submission of a certificate evidencing liability insurance coverage as set forth in paragraph 9, and (E) a request for an interim payment: $_____.

(c) Effect of Approval for Interim Payment. Approval of the work to permit an interim payment is solely for the benefit of the Artist. Unless the approval of the work is in the form of a resolution by the Commission, the approval does not constitute acceptance or approval of the work by the City nor shall it be construed as a waiver of the City's right to require that the work conform strictly to the Proposal and to the specifications set forth in subparagraph 1(a).

(d) Final Acceptance by the City. The work shall be finally accepted by the City when the Commission adopts a resolution finding:

(i) that the work conforms to the Proposal and specifications set forth in subparagraph 1(a) hereof, or to any modifications thereof approved by resolution of the Commission;

(ii) that the Artist transported the work to and installed the work at the site on a timely basis, or that the Commission for good cause waived the City's right to so require; and

(iii) that the Artist is in substantial compliance with the other terms of this agreement which the Commission has not waived.

(e) Waiver of Final Acceptance. If the Artist is in all other respects in compliance with the terms of this agreement, the City shall be deemed to have waived:

(i) the Artist's obligation to transport and install the work at the site, if the Artist is not given access to the site for installation by _____; or

(ii) the right to reject the work as not conforming to the Proposal or the specifications set forth in paragraph 1(a), if the work is accessible within 20 miles of the City for review by the Commission and the Commission fails to determine by _____ whether or not the work conforms to the Proposal and specifications as provided for in subparagraph 4(d)(i). The Artist may relinquish the right to enforce the foregoing waivers in a dated, signed writing.

(f) Waiver of Installation. If for any reason the Commission waives the Artist's obligation to transport and install the work at the site, $_____, which represents the anticipated savings to the Artist, shall be deducted from the fee otherwise payable pursuant to subparagraph 4(a).

(g) Refund of Interim Payments. If the City terminates this agreement pursuant to paragraph 24, the Artist must refund the interim payments.

6. Indemnification. The Artist agrees to defend, indemnify and hold harmless the City, its members, officers, agents and employees, from and against all claims, costs and damages arising out of the Artist's activities under this agreement.

7. Artist's Warranties.

(a) Defects in Material or Workmanship and Inherent Vice. The Artist warrants that the work will be free of defects in workmanship or materials, including inherent vice, and that the Artist will, at the Artist's own expense, remedy any defects due to faulty workmanship or materials, or to inherent vice, which appear within a period of three years from the date the work is finally accepted by the City. If the work should deteriorate because of an inherent vice between three and fifteen years from the date the work is finally accepted by the City, the Artist will repair or replace the work for the cost of materials and supplies. "Inherent vice" refers to a quality within the material or materials which comprise the work which, either alone or in combination, results in the tendency of the work to destroy itself. "Inherent vice" does not include any tendency to deteriorate which is specifically identified in the Proposal submitted by the Artist.

(b) Public Safety. The Artist warrants that the work will not contain sharp points or edges which the Commission deems a danger to the public and agrees to cooperate in making or permitting adjustments to the work if necessary to eliminate other hazards which become apparent within one year of the date the work is finally accepted by the City.

(c) Title. The Artist warrants that the work is the result of the artistic efforts of the Artist and that it will be installed free and clear of any liens, claims or other encumbrances of any type.

(d) Unique. The Artist warrants that the work is unique and an edition of one, and that the Artist will not execute or authorize another to execute another work of the same design, dimensions and materials as the work commissioned pursuant to this agreement. For the purposes of this warranty, if the dimensions of another work exceed 75% of the dimensions of the commissioned work, the other work shall be deemed to be of the same dimensions as the commissioned work. This warranty shall continue in effect for a period consisting of the life of the Artist plus 50 years and shall be binding on the Artist's heirs and assigns.

8. Excuse or Suspension of Contractual Obligations. The parties shall be excused from performing any obligation under this agreement if performance of that obligation is prevented by a condition beyond the control of the parties, such as acts of God, war, public emergency, or strike or other labor disturbance. An obligation affected by a condition beyond the control of the parties shall be suspended only for the duration of the condition. Both parties shall take all reasonable steps during the existence of the condition to assure performance of their contractual obligations when the condition no longer exists.

9. Claims, Mediation and Arbitration.
(a) Claims. Each claim against the City arising out of this Agreement shall be submitted to the Controller of the City within 100 days of the time that the cause of action arises. Any claim expressly denied or deemed denied by the City may be submitted to mediation or arbitration as provided in subsection (b).

(b) Mediation and Arbitration. The parties may submit disputes or claims arising under this agreement to mediation or nonbinding arbitration. For this purpose, the parties may utilize the services of the Arts Arbitration and Mediation Services, a program of California Lawyers for the Arts, or some other service acceptable to the parties.

10. Insurance.
(a) Type, Amount, and Duration. The Artist shall:
(i) Procure and maintain throughout the fabrication, transportation and installation phases of this agreement, worker's compensation insurance and employer's liability insurance, with

limits of no less than $1 million each accident. If the Artist has no employees as defined by state law, and the Artist submits a letter so stating, this requirement may be waived in writing by the Commission.

(ii) Procure and maintain until the work is installed by the Artist and custody relinquished to the City, fine arts insurance on an all risk form with limits not less than $_____ and deductible not to exceed $1,000 each loss, with any loss payable to the City as its interests may appear.

(iii) Procure prior to requesting the second interim payment, or entering the site for the purpose of installing the work, whichever occurs earlier, maintain until the work is accepted by the City:

(A) General liability insurance with limits of not less than $1 million each occurrence, combined single limit bodily injury and property damage, including coverage for contractual liability, broad form property damage, completed operations and, if any subcontracted work, independent contractors.

(B) Automobile liability insurance with limits not less than $1 million each occurrence combined single limit for bodily injury and property damage, including coverages for owned, non-owned and hired vehicles, as applicable.

(b) Endorsements. Automobile and general liability insurance shall be endorsed to:

(i) Name as additional insureds the City and the Committee, and their officers, agents and employees.

(ii) Provide that the policies are primary insurance to any other insurance available to the additional insureds, with respect to claims arising out of this agreement, and that the insurance applies separately to each insured against whom claim is made or suit is brought.

(iii) Provide 45 days advance written notice of cancellation, non renewal or reduction in coverage mailed to:

_____

_____

_____

(c) Certificate. Certificates of insurance evidencing worker's compensation and fine arts coverages and worker's endorsements set forth above shall be furnished to the City prior to certification of this agreement by the Controller. Certificates of insurance evidencing the liability coverages and endorsements set forth above shall be furnished to the City at the time of the Artist's request for the second interim payment, or of the Artist's request for access to the site for installation of the work, whichever may occur earlier. Upon request certified copies of all policies shall be furnished to the City.

(d) Fine Arts After Installation. The City shall procure and maintain fine arts insurance on the work on an all-risk form with limits not less than $ _____, and deductible not to exceed $ _____ each loss, from the time the work is installed at the site and the Artist relinquishes custody to the City, until the work is finally accepted by the City and the fee is paid to the Artist. The Artist shall be named as an additional insured on the policy. A certificate of insurance evidencing such coverage shall be furnished to the Artist upon request.

11. Copyright.

(a) General. The Artist shall place a copyright notice on the work in the form and manner required to protect copyrights in the work under United States copyright law. If the copyright is registered with the U.S. Copyright Office, the artist shall provide the City with a copy of the application for registration, the registration number and the effective date of registration. Except as provided in this agreement, the Artist retains all copyrights in the work.

(b) Display. The Artist hereby grants the City the exclusive right to display the work and to loan the work to other persons or institutions with authority to display it publicly.

(c) Reproductions. The Artist hereby authorizes the City to make, and to authorize the making of, photographs and other two-dimensional reproductions of the work for educational, public relations, arts promotional and other noncommercial purposes. For the purposes of this agreement, the following are deemed to be reproductions for noncommercial purposes: reproduction in exhibition catalogues, books, slides, photographs, postcards, posters; and calendars; in art magazines, art books and art and news sections of newspapers; in general books and magazines not primarily devoted to art but of an educational, historical or critical nature; slides and film strips not intended for a mass audience; and television from stations operated for educational purposes or on programs for educational purposes from all stations. On any and all such reproductions, the City shall place a copyright notice in the form and manner required to protect the copyrights in the works under the United States copyright law.

(d) Royalties on Posters. The City shall pay to the Artist 50% of any royalty which the City receives from the sale of poster reproductions of the work in excess of 7500 copies. If the City makes poster reproductions itself, it shall pay to the Artist a royalty of 15% on the net wholesale price from the sale of reproductions in excess of 7500 copies. For the purposes of this section, the "net wholesale price" is the wholesale billing price to customers or distributors less customary discounts and allowances actually allowed and less any returns and transportation charges allowed on returns. The Artist is responsible for keeping the Commission informed of his or her current address, and the City shall mail notice of any amount due hereunder to the Artist annually at his or her last known address. The right to any royalty not claimed within three years from the date of the annual notice to the Artist reverts to the City.

12. Credits.

(a) Label. A label identifying the Artist, the title of the work and the year it is completed shall be publicly displayed in the area adjacent to the work.

(b) Artist's Credit. The City agrees that unless the Artist requests to the contrary in writing, all references to the work and all reproductions of the work shall credit the work to the Artist.

(c) City's Credit. The Artist agrees that all formal references to the work shall include the following credit line: "From the Collection of the City [Building], commissioned through the Committee."

13. Documentation. The Artist shall provide information on the work requested by the Commission for its registration files. The City shall provide the Artist with one 35-mm color slide of the work, accurate in color and detail, after the work has been installed.

14. Repair and Restoration. It is the policy of the Commission to consult with an Artist regarding repairs and restoration which are undertaken during the Artist's lifetime when that is practicable. To facilitate consultation, Artist will, to the extent feasible, notify the Commission of any change in permanent address.

15. California Art Preservation Act. A copy of the California Art Preservation Act, Section 987 of the California Civil Code, which generally prohibits the physical defacement, mutilation, alteration or destruction of a work of fine art by anyone other than the Artist, appears as Exhibit A hereto for reference by the parties.

16. Reputation.

(a) City's Commitment. The City agrees that it will not use the work or the Artist's name in a way which reflects discredit on the work or on the name of the Artist or on the reputation of the Artist as an artist.

(b) Artist's Commitment. The Artist agrees that Artist will not make reference to the work or reproduce the work, or any portion thereof, in a way which reflects discredit on the City or the work.

17. Return of Work. If the Commission removes the work permanently from the site within three years of the date of this agreement, the Commission shall give the Artist prompt notice of the removal. The work will be returned to the Artist and the City will waive its right to make additional reproductions of the work if the Artist refunds to the City the fee paid pursuant to this agreement within 60 days of receiving notice of the removal and pays all of the expenses related to the return.

18. Title and Risk of Loss. Title to the work passes to the City when the fee is paid to the Artist. The Artist bears the risk of damage to or loss of the work until title passes to the City.

19. No Assignment or Transfer. The personal skill, judgment and creativity of the Artist is an essential element of this agreement. Therefore, although the parties recognize that the Artist may employ qualified personnel to work under Artist's supervision, the Artist shall not assign, transfer or subcontract the creative and artistic portions of the work to another party without the prior written consent of the City.

20. Artist as Independent Contractor. The Artist shall perform all work under this agreement as an independent contractor and not as an agent or an employee of the City.

21. Employment Non-Discrimination. The provisions of Section 12.B 2 of the City Administrative Code are attached hereto as Exhibit B and incorporated herein.

22. Amendments. No modification or amendment of the terms of this agreement shall be effective unless written and signed by authorized representatives of the parties hereto.

23. Governing Law. This agreement and all matters pertaining thereto shall be construed according to the laws of the State of California.

24. Budget and Fiscal Provisions of Charter. This agreement is subject to the budget and fiscal provisions of the City's Charter. Charges will accrue only after the City's Controller certifies that funds are available for the City's obligation under the agreement. The amount of the City's obligation under this agreement shall not exceed the amount certified as available for the purposes in the agreement. This section shall control against any and all other provisions of this agreement.

25. Remedies for Violation of Terms of Agreement.

(a) The remedy described in subparagraph (b) is in addition to all other remedies available to either party under the laws of the State of California should the other party fail to comply with the terms of this agreement.

(b) The City may terminate this agreement if the work as fabricated does not conform to the Proposal and the specifications as provided in paragraph 1(a) hereof. The agreement shall be deemed terminated 60 days after the Commission delivers to the Artist a notice of intent to terminate. The notice shall specify the grounds for termination. The Commission may rescind the notice or extend the date for termination, but no rescission or extension is valid unless it is in writing and approved by resolution of the Commission. If the agreement is terminated pursuant to this paragraph, the Artist shall refund any interim payments which have been made.

26. Notices. Submittals, requests, notices and reports required under this agreement shall be delivered as follows:

For the Artist: _____

_____

_____

_____

For the Commission: _____

_____

_____

_____

A change in the designation of the person or address to which submittals, requests, notices and reports shall be delivered is effective when the other party has received notice of the change by certified mail.

ART COMMISSION   ARTIST

By _____   By _____

_____, Director   Social Security No. _____

APPROVED AS TO FORM: APPROVED:

_____, City Attorney   _____

Purchaser of Supplies

By _____

City Attorney

The following pages contain a "Form VA" from the United States Copyright Office. Original forms are available free of charge from the Copyright Office.

FORM VA
UNITED STATES COPYRIGHT OFFICE

REGISTRATION NUMBER

VA   VAU

EFFECTIVE DATE OF REGISTRATION

Month   Day   Year

DO NOT WRITE ABOVE THIS LINE. IF YOU NEED MORE SPACE, USE A SEPARATE CONTINUATION SHEET.

1   **TITLE OF THIS WORK** ▼   NATURE OF THIS WORK ▼ See instructions

PREVIOUS OR ALTERNATIVE TITLES ▼

PUBLICATION AS A CONTRIBUTION If this work was published as a contribution to a periodical, serial, or collection, give information about the collective work in which the contribution appeared.   **Title of Collective Work** ▼

If published in a periodical or serial give: Volume ▼   Number ▼   Issue Date ▼   On Pages ▼

2   **a**   **NAME OF AUTHOR** ▼

DATES OF BIRTH AND DEATH
Year Born ▼   Year Died ▼

Was this contribution to the work a "work made for hire"?

☐ Yes
☐ No

AUTHOR'S NATIONALITY OR DOMICILE
Name of Country

OR { Citizen of ▶
    Domiciled in ▶

WAS THIS AUTHOR'S CONTRIBUTION TO THE WORK

Anonymous?   ☐ Yes ☐ No
Pseudonymous? ☐ Yes ☐ No

If the answer to either of these questions is "Yes," see detailed instructions.

NOTE

Under the law, the "author" of a "work made for hire" is generally the employer, not the employee (see instructions). For any part of this work that was "made for hire" check "Yes" in the space provided, give the employer (or other person for whom the work was prepared) as "Author" of that part, and leave the space for dates of birth and death blank.

NATURE OF AUTHORSHIP Briefly describe nature of the material created by this author in which copyright is claimed. ▼

b **NAME OF AUTHOR** ▼

DATES OF BIRTH AND DEATH
Year Born ▼   Year Died ▼

Was this contribution to the work a "work made for hire"?
☐ Yes
☐ No

AUTHOR'S NATIONALITY OR DOMICILE
Name of country
OR { Citizen of ▶
     Domiciled in ▶

WAS THIS AUTHOR'S CONTRIBUTION TO THE WORK
Anonymous?   ☐ Yes ☐ No
Pseudonymous?   ☐ Yes ☐ No
If the answer to either of these questions is "Yes," see detailed instructions.

NATURE OF AUTHORSHIP Briefly describe nature of the material created by this author in which copyright is claimed. ▼

c **NAME OF AUTHOR** ▼

DATES OF BIRTH AND DEATH
Year Born ▼   Year Died ▼

Was this contribution to the work a "work made for hire"?
☐ Yes
☐ No

AUTHOR'S NATIONALITY OR DOMICILE
Name of Country
OR { Citizen of ▶
     Domiciled in ▶

WAS THIS AUTHOR'S CONTRIBUTION TO THE WORK
Anonymous?   ☐ Yes ☐ No
Pseudonymous?   ☐ Yes ☐ No
If the answer to either of these questions is "Yes," see detailed instructions.

NATURE OF AUTHORSHIP Briefly describe nature of the material created by this author in which copyright is claimed. ▼

3 **YEAR IN WHICH CREATION OF THIS WORK WAS COMPLETED** This information must be given in all cases.
◀ Year

DATE AND NATION OF FIRST PUBLICATION OF THIS PARTICULAR WORK
Complete this information ONLY if this work has been published.
Month ▶   Day ▶   Year ▶   ◀ Nation

4 **COPYRIGHT CLAIMANT(S)** Name and address must be given even if the claimant is the same as the author given in space 2. ▼

TRANSFER If the claimant(s) named here in space 4 are different from the author(s) named in space 2, give a brief statement of how the claimant(s) obtained ownership of the copyright. ▼

See instructions before completing this space.

**DO NOT WRITE HERE
OFFICE USE ONLY**

APPLICATION RECEIVED

ONE DEPOSIT RECEIVED

TWO DEPOSITS RECEIVED

REMITTANCE NUMBER AND DATE

MORE ON BACK ▶
• Complete all applicable spaces (numbers 5-9) on the reverse side of this page.
• See detailed instructions.
• Sign the form at line 8.

DO NOT WRITE HERE
Page 1 of _____ pages

EXAMINED BY

CHECKED BY

☐ CORRESPONDENCE
   Yes

☐ DEPOSIT ACCOUNT
   FUNDS USED

FORM VA

FOR
COPYRIGHT
OFFICE
USE
ONLY

DO NOT WRITE ABOVE THIS LINE. IF YOU NEED MORE SPACE, USE A SEPARATE CONTINUATION SHEET.

PREVIOUS REGISTRATION Has registration for this work, or for an earlier version of this work, already been made in the Copyright Office?

☐ Yes ☐ No If your answer is "Yes," why is another registration being sought? (Check appropriate box) ▼

☐ This is the first published edition of a work previously registered in unpublished form.

☐ This is the first application submitted by this author as copyright claimant.

☐ This is a changed version of the work, as shown by space 6 on this application.

If your answer is "Yes," give: **Previous Registration Number** ▼   **Year of Registration** ▼

5

DERIVATIVE WORK OR COMPILATION Complete both space 6a & 6b for a derivative work; complete only 6b for a compilation. ▼

a. **Preexisting Material** Identify any preexisting work or works that this work is based on or incorporates. ▼

b. **Material Added to This Work** Give a brief, general statement of the material that has been added to this work and in which copyright is claimed. ▼

6

See instructions
before completing
this space.

DEPOSIT ACCOUNT If the registration fee is to be charged to a Deposit Account established in the Copyright Office, give name and number of Account.

Name ▼   **Account Number** ▼

7

CORRESPONDENCE Give name and address to which correspondence about this application should be sent. Name/Address/Apt/City/State/Zip ▼

Area Code & Telephone Number ▼

Be sure to
give your
daytime phone
▼ number.

8

CERTIFICATION* I, the undersigned, hereby certify that I am the

Check only one ▼

☐ author
☐ other copyright claimant
☐ owner of exclusive right(s)
☐ authorized agent of _____
Name of author or other copyright claimant, or owner of exclusive right(s) ▲

of the work identified in this application and that the statements made
by me in this application are correct to the best of my knowledge.

Typed or printed name and date ▼ If this is a published work, this date must be the same as or later than the date of publication given in space 3.

_____ date ▶ _____

☛ Handwritten signature (X) ▼

MAIL CERTIFI-CATE TO

Name ▼

Number/Street/Apartment Number ▼

City/State/ZIP ▼

Certificate will be mailed in window envelope

9

Have you:

● Completed all necessary spaces?
● Signed your application in space 8?
● Enclosed check or money order for $10 payable to *Register of Copyrights?*
● Enclosed your deposit material with the application and fee?

MAIL TO: Register of Copyrights, Library of Congress, Washington, D.C. 20559.

☆U.S. GOVERNMENT PRINTING OFFICE: 1987—181—531/60,009

August 1987—60,000

INDEX

138 • *Index*